Angels of the Lord

רב ־ מ־לאך-מַלְאַך

An apostolic-prophetic-messianic teaching

by

Dr. Gunter Rappl

Ekklesia Consuming Fire & GFC, Cologne, Germany

Bibliographische Information der Deutschen Nationalbibliothek:

Die Deutsche Nationalbibliothek verzeichnet diese Publikation in der deutschen Nationalbibliographie; detalierte biographische Daten sind im Internet über http://dnb.dnd.de abrufbar.

Ekklesia Consuming Fire & GFC

Woehlerstrasse 16 A

50823 Cologne, Germany

Contact: g.rappl@ekklesia-koeln.de

© 2018

Herstellung und Verlag: BoD - Books on Demand, Norderstedt, Deutschland.

2018 Erste Ausgabe

ISBN: 978-3-3748-1841-95

Dedication

The teaching course and both books are dedicated first and foremost to the glory of YHWH Echad. Without your salvation and the restoration of my life into chaim life, this School of Angels manual would not have been possible.

Special thanks to Kay Tolman and Jeff Jansen for believing in YHWH's calling on my life and overshadowing in prayer and intercession my sonship so that I could mature more and more into Yeshua's glory.

Special thanks to Kevin Basconi and Christine Pruitt for rapid help, their prayers, and for Kevin's new training manual about angelic ministry so that I could include the revelations it contains in this school. Angels find everything that has been held up at customs or at post offices!

Special thanks also to the members and visitors of Ekklesia Consuming Fire & GFC Cologne, Germany. Your hunger and thirst for the deeper things of YHWH motivated me to search the scriptures, literature and revelations so that I could put together this manual and school. May angels be your fellow servants and friends!

A special thanks to Nicole Sametat, for inspiring discussions as well as shared journeys into the supernatural, meeting a lot of different angels in the heavens, the court- and council rooms.

Special thanks to Manfred and Janet Meyer for proofreading the manuscript, and helpful suggestions for the style and format of this book.

Let us all come into maturity and our calling to see awakening and revival in our meetings, in celebrating the moedim of the Lord, on the seven mountains of society, in cities, in regions and in the nations all over the world!

Heb. 6: 1-3: "Therefore leaving the principles of the doctrine of the Mashiach, let us go on unto maturity; not laying again the foundation of repentance from dead works, and of faith toward God, of the doctrine of baptisms, and of laying on of hands, and of resurrection of the dead, and of eternal judgement. And this will we do, if God permits."

Dr. Gunter Rappl, in the month of Adar II, 5776.
Manual and book finished August 31, 2016.

Endorsements

• Prophet Jan Jansen, Global Fire Ministries (Jeff Jansen): "Awesome that you have written this Gunter! That is awesome! You just keep doing what you do!"

• Pastor Kay Tolman, Restoration Gateway Ministries: "I'm very excited to review this material. Congratulations on completing it."

• Christine Pruitt, King of Glory Ministries International (Kevin Basconi): "Praise the Lord for this manual!"

• Seer Justin Abraham, Company of Burning Hearts: "Very well done with your school. You did a very good job pulling all the information together."

• Seer Kathy Madden, Creative Blue Light Beings: "This manual contains many everlasting fruitful blessings for the reader."

• Commentary of a participant of the "School of Angels" in Portland, OR, USA in September 2016: "The September School of Angels by Apostle Dr. Gunter Rappl was astounding. With great revelatory style, Gunter detailed the various types and functions of angels and encouraged us to look for them everywhere."

• A German Messianic leader/publisher: "The author has invested a lot of time to put together all the material about angels of YHWH Echad, which even I don't know in detail. For persons not solid in English language, I can say, as soon as the book is available in German language, I would directly purchase and read it."

• A Personal note from the author: „Shortly before the submission of both books to the publisher my computer started to get problems with the windows and bios system. So through YHWH Echad's mercy and grace it was possible for me to backup up everything on my computer, before a computer specialist must delete all files on my harddrive so that my computer could run again with a new installed windows and bios system. I'm so thankful to YHWH Echad that nothing of the material in both books was lost, so the body of the Mashiach can purchase, read and judge it."

Proofreading of the manuscript: Manfred and Janet Meyer, Glory World Media, 46509 Xanten, Germany

Bible Versions

All Bible scripture used in this publication is mainly from the online King James Version of the Bible (2012), but I compared the Bible passages cited in this book with translations from other Bible versions, listed below. I used all the different Bible versions, the Bible Dictionary, or Hebrew and Greek Concordances by permission from the publishers.

My Bible on-line program with Bible versions: © 2012. By myBible.ink.

- King James Version, KJV with Apocrypha
- Elberfelder 1905 with Strong's Concordance
- Schlachter 2000
- Luther, new translation

- Strong's Concordance Hebrew © 1890. By James Strong, Madison, NJ.
- Strong's Concordance Greek © 1890. By James Strong, Madison, NJ.
- Eastons Bible Dictionary © 1897. Illustrated Bible Dictionary, Third Edition, published by Thomas Nelson.

- Complete Jewish Bible © 1998. David H. Stern.
- Hebraic Roots Bible © 2012. Word of Truth Publications.
- One New Man Bible © 2011. William J. Morford.
- Orthodox Jewish Bible © 2011. Artists For Israel Intl Inc.
- Restoration Study Bible © 2006. Your Arms To Yisrael Publishing.
- The Power New Testament © 2011. William J. Morford.
- The Hebraic-Roots Version Scriptures, Revised Edition © 2009. James Scott Trimm.

- Interlinear Bible for Old and New Testament © 2011. Biblica Hebraica Stuttgartensia, Deutsche Bibelgesellschaft, Stuttgart.

- Septuagint Bible in English © 1851. Samuel Bagster & Sons, Ltd., London.
- Luther Bible with Apocrypha, new translation © 1999. Deutsche Bibelgesellschaft, Stuttgart.
- New International Version © 2011. Zondervan, USA
- New Living Translation © 2016. Tyndale House Publishers, USA

Seventh expanded and revised version, fall ([Heb.] "*Stav*" = season of repentance),
1. Tishrei (Begin of returning to YHWH Echad), *Yom Teru'ah* 5779

Contents (Boot camp)

Contents (Boot camp)

Introduction

Are Angels real, do they exist today, are they minister to humans? In this book you find answers you never dared to asked other believers. I, Gunter, was in interaction with angels all the days of my life, often I didn't know it, praise YHWH Echad for his mercy and grace.

During my journey into Yeshua's freedom, YHWH Echad has developed in me the gift of discernment for His glory so I can discern different fallen angels and demons.

Last year I felt in my heart, that the Ruach HaKodesh spoke to me, to teach a school of angels in my ekklesia/edah and so I started to collect informations and got revelations by YHWH Echad and put them all together in the book, you hold in your hands now, and in book 2 of this series. During my hunger and thirst for deeper revelations about the angels of Yeshua, I realized, that I found more and more angels with specific names and functions, mentioned in the Bible or other jewish scriptures, including the apocryphal texts, not included in most of the "classical Bible versions."

Now I think with this gift of discernment in me I have listed and described over 300 different angels in book 1 and 2 of this series, compared to the two or three normally known by believers, e.g. *Michael, Gabriel* and *Raphael*. By the way, there are myriads of angels and archangels ministering under the rule and dominon of YHWH Echad, so even the number 300+ is only a small description of the whole angelic realm. But it is most important to discern angels correctly, as angels of the Lord or not, together with all the different functions angels of the Lord will help the believers in their walk of faith. The reason I believe that our God revealed the understanding of the angelic realm to me was my love, prayer and support for our roots, the good olive tree, the nation of Israel and my openness to trust the Ruach HaKodesh to lead me to apocryphal scriptures, where, like it is recommended for prophecies, you must test everything and to take hold of the good. My special thanks goes to Apostle Dale M. Sides for encouraging me to read apocryphal scripture. The angels of YHWH normally speak Hebrew language, but praise God, you can speak to them with your native language and they understand you, because in the training school of angels in heaven, they are taught the 70 languages of the first nations of the earth and so they can understand also dialects of these 70 languages.

Dear reader, as I learned to grow into the understanding of the angelic realm, I trust YHWH Echad, that you also grow into the discernment of them. So I hope you enjoy this book and apply everything you learn therein by the Ruach HaKodesh for YHWH's glory. "And don't forget, now is the season of the angels of YHWH Echad (Perry Stone, This Season of Angels, 2018)."

Shalom! Dr. Gunter Rappl, Apostle Ekklesia Consuming Fire & GFC Cologne, Germany.

School of Angelic Ministry (Boot camp)

Illustration: **The Angel of the Lord** ("*Malakh Elohim*," e.g. here *Chamuel* [Pers. Rev. GR]) **wrestling with Jacob** (Gen. 32:24-25), **by Gustave Dore**. **Dore's English Bible, public domain**.

"Are they not all ministering spirits, sent forth to minister to them who shall be heirs of salvation? (Heb. 1:14)."

Angels

This teaching establishes a biblical foundation for the evidence for and ministry of angels:

Topics include:

- **What are angels?**
- **Dimensions of heaven**
- **Ministry of angels**
- **Types of angels**
- **Functions of angels**
- **Characteristics of angels**
- **Hierarchy**
- Specific angels/angel names

Book 1/ Boot camp Level

Book 2/ Advanced Level

Shadow type style: *Rabbinic belief, Jewish Messianic belief*, and book *"Legends of the Jews."*

Abbreviations:

GR = Gunter Rappl

Ap. = Apostle

Proph. = Prophet

Pers. Rev. = Personal revelation

Heb. = Hebrew

OT = Old Testament

NT = New Testament

Gr. = Greek

A.D. = Anno Domini

Names of God (YHWH Echad):

In this book the *original hebrew names* of the God of Israel (YHWH Echad) are used: *Elohim Avinu* as God the **Father**, *Yeshua HaMashiach* as the **Son** of the Living God, and *Ruach HaKodesh* as the **Spirit**/Breath of God.

Angels: Basic understanding

➢ **Angels** (*"angelos"* [Gr.], *"malak"* [Heb.]): ***"messenger," "one going."***

➢ **Angels** are mentioned in 17 OT and 17 NT books, **in total over 250 times in the Bible.**

➢ **The most reliable information about angels is found in the Bible, the most detailed information on them in the Apocrypha** (e.g. *Enoch, Book of Jubilees, Books of Ezra, Gospel of Bartholomew, Revelation of Peter, Apocalypse of Paul, Book of Jashar*, etc.). The books of the **Apocrypha** were written in the **2ⁿᵈ temple period** and in **early Edah time** until 400 A.D.. Messianic bible teacher **Dr. Michael Heiser** has **published** 2016 a great **teaching** (available as PDF download from his website) **showing** that the **writers** of the **NT knew OT Apocrypha.**

➢ *Legends of the Jews*: "Angels are generally divided (according to their assignments) into, ***ministering angels*** (*"Malakhei Ha-Sharet,"* [Heb.]) and the **angels of praise** or *glory* (*"Zamarim,"* [Heb.])."

➢ For **everything** there is an **angel assigned**: "For every **individual**, for every **family**, for every **ekklesia/edah**, for every **city**, for every **nation** and for every **tectonic plate** (Proph. Ian Clayton, Realms of the Kingdom Vol. 2, 2016)." There is **a hierarchy** and **order among the angels**. "YHWH Echad commanded that all the angels should assemble in His presence, **each in his order**," (*Apoc. Moses* 39:2).

➢ *"Familiar angels"* are **"activated"** when the **bloodline of one believer of** the **family line is cleansed** by the blood of Yeshua. Then, *familiar angels* help the **Ruach HaKodesh**, so that **all other family members**, if they are **not saved yet, get saved** (see Acts 16:31). *Familiar angels* interact with **YHWH Echad** of their **own initiative** to **petition Him for other angels to be dispatched** to **minister** to the **family line.**

Why do we need to understand the ministry of Angels?

➢ *Angels* and ***mankind should work together in the army of the Lord*** (2 Chron. 32:20-21 [the angel *Remiel* was sent by YHWH Echad as help for Israel, {GR}], *War Rules XII*, Dead Sea scrolls [instructions for Israel to go to battle]); **men is in hierarchy over angels** (but *lower than God*, [Heb.] *"Elohiyim"*) (see Ps. 8:5) (more about the hierarchy of mankind in relation to YHWH Echad and angels see *"order in the army,"* **page 8**).

➢ **Two sides of interaction with angels:**

o **Satanic trap: Todd Bentley** and **"Emma O angel"** at *Lakeland revival* 2006. Todd didn't recognize fallen angel "of Japan mythology" (even mentioned in *Wikipedia* as goddess) masquerading as an *angel of light* at Lakeland revival 2006 (for *angel of light* see 2 Cor. 11:14, *Apoc. Moses* 17:2). The result was that **Satan robbed** a lot of the **good godly fruits of this revival** which had drawn worldwide attention because of unusual **signs, wonders** and **miracles** performed by the **hand of YHWH Echad**. Additionally **Todd Bentley's ministry** had to **be restored** by YHWH Echad after Lakeland revival **of all things which went wrong there**. (How to **guard** and **deliver yourself against/from deception** see **page 16**).

Ref.: Greg Crawford, Angels Helping Us Contend, 2013; Douglas Connelly, Angels Around Us, 1994

Events in the history of the Ekklesia/Edah influencing interaction with angels (I)

- At the Council of Niceae around **300 A.D.** Emperor Constantin set in order **state religion** and **priesthood** (**not pastors**) (founded in *Mithraism*). He **removed** the **structure of Ekklesia/Edah** and the "**five fold ministry**" and **didn't allowed some books** of Jewish origin, some are even mentioned in the Bible (like *Enoch* and *Jashar*) **to be considered inspired word of God**. Especially the three books of *Enoch* teach a lot about angels and their ministry.

- At **590 A.D.** Pope Gregory the great banished the original "Solfeggio tones" given by **YHWH Echad** to the **nation of Israel**, at the **times of David, for temple worship**, because "the intervals (the frequencies) were too Holy for the ears of man." By the **year 1050 A.D.**, the **Edah** admitted to **losing 152** of the **original Solfeggios** sung **by the early Edah** prior to Pope Gregory (Michael S. Tyrell, Wholetones: The Sound of Healing, 2014).

The *worship angels (Zamarim)* **in heaven compose worship music** with **this "Solfeggio tones"** (there are 12 main "Solfeggio frequencies"). The *worship angels* **playing instruments**, often made out of Cedar wood, like David made instruments of Cedar wood, which **emit very warm** and **beautiful tones, sounding** as well as **delightfully aromatic**. In addition there are **12 specific colors associated** with the **12 main "Solfeggio tones," supporting** the **effects** of the **worship music** on the **hearer/worshipper**. The **12 main "Solfeggio tones"** and their **associated 12 colors** are **linked** to the **12 tribes of Israel** (Pers. Rev. GR, for more details see book 2). The **archangel** and **his angel army** which was **comissioned by YHWH Echad** to **protect** and **guard** a **specific tribe of Israel** is **associated/ "drawn"** with/ to the **specific color** and the **specific "Solfeggio frequency"** of the **tribe** (Pers. Rev. GR, for more details about angels and "Solfeggio frequencies"see book 2).

The "Solfeggio frequencies" are **correlated** with the **numerical values** of the **hebrew letters** of the **furniture** for the **Tabernacle of YHWH** and **they are found in Numbers 7:12-83, Genesis** (in the first chapters), the **Psalms of David** (Ps. 120-134, some say also in Ps. 135) and **Joshua ch. 6** (Shir Le, Tabernacle Prayer Frequencies of Power, 2015; Dr. Leonard Horowitz, Healing Codes for the Biological Apocalypse, 1999). **YHWH Echad released** through this **worship music deliverance, restoration** and **healing** into the **hearers/worshippers** because *deliverance angels*, *angels of healing* or *angels of restoration* (for more details about these *angel groups* see book 2 of this series) of **YHWH Echad** were **activated by** the **music**. Read for the scriptural proof of this statement in 1 Sam. 16:23: "When David played, **the evil spirit left King Saul** and his peace returned" (**only angels of YHWH Echad** can **defeat evil spirits**, [GR]). David's playing was so effective that King Saul asked David's father, Jesse, if David could stay in his service. It is written **in the Bible** that **whenever** an **evil spirit tormented King Saul, David would play** and **the spirit would leave** (because of **angelic ministry** of **angels** of **HaShem El Israel**, [GR]).

Tammy Sorenson published 2018 an instrumental CD **with "Solfeggio frequencies"** bringing specific **healing to trauma**. The "**Solfeggio frequencies**" which she used **under inspiration** of the **Ruach HaKodesh** are *396 Hz, 444 Hz, 528 Hz,* and *741 Hz*. These "**Solfeggio frequencies**" specifically **activate** *Seraphim, Benai Elohim, Cherubim* and *Irim* angels (Pers. Rev. GR).

Events in the history of the Ekklesia/Edah influencing interaction with angels (II)

These **four angel groups** are **especially responsible** for bringing **deliverance, healing** and **restoration** to saints in **body, soul,** and **spirit** (Pers. Rev. GR). **Praise YHWH Echad** for the **worldwide restoration** of the **usage** of "**Solfeggio frequencies**" in the Edah of Yeshua (GR).

David van Koevering and **John Tussey** compose worship music with the **music frequencies** of the **31 elements** with **which YHWH Echad created mankind**. The **sounds of these 31 elements are heard** by **prophets of HaShem** in the **dimensions of heaven** (John Tussey, 2016). These "*Frequencies of Creation*" attract *healing angels* of **YHWH Echad** and **release healing** upon mankind on a **quantum mechanical** or **quantum physics level. Tammy Sorenson** uses a **computer program "Bible Music Writer"** from **Uri Harel to translate words of the Bible in tones/music for worship** and **healing through activation** of *angels of healing* and *restoration* of **YHWH Echad**. The **22 letters** of the **hebrew "Aleph-Beth"** are connected to **healing** of **specific body parts** (Dr. Pamela Legate, Blessing Your Body, 2017).

- In **741 A.D.**, there was a **monk**, for whom it was **normal** to **engage** in his life, and the life of the ekklesia/edah of which he was a part, **190 realms of different angels, known by name** and **function** (Proph. Ian Clayton). At the Council of Rome in **745 A.D.**, the Catholic Church **forbade under threat of excommunication** the *knowing* and *reverencing* of any other than the **three angels** *Michael, Gabriel,* and *Raphael* (Feast of Veneration of Archangels in Catholic Church, celebrated on Sept. 29). YHWH **forbid** the **worship of angels** (Col. 2:18)!!!

- The common **personal use of anointing oil** continued **until the 9th century**. Around that time, the **church rituals** and **church rules** arose, and the **common personal use of anointing oil declined** until the **personal use vanished completely** in the **9th century**. Instead, the **anointing oil was only** to be **used by** the **church leaders**. We're talking about the early **Catholic Church. The Catholic Church had established defined anointing rites**, and **only for the anointing of** the **sick people**. After the Great Schism, and **a century before the Reformation**, it **even became worse**. From that moment the Catholic Church leaders decided that **anointing was no longer for the sick**, but only **for those who were about to die (like** the **funeral rites in ancient Egypt** or **other cults of the world**, [GR]). So if you were sick, **you had to wait until you were dying** before **one of** the **Catholic Church leaders** was even willing to **come** and **anoint you**. So one key, e.g. **anointing oil**, to **activate angels** was **lost in the 9th century** by the Ekklesia/Edah. (Robin Prijs, The Anointed Bride, 2016).

Each tribe of Israel also **has a specific anointing oil** (Pers. Rev. GR). For more about **angels** and **anointing** or **fragrance oils** see **book 2** of this series. The **importance of anointing oils** is demonstrated by the fact, that **the Bible refers to essential oils** or **aromatic plants** and **products 1035 times!** (Dr. David Stewart, Healing Oils of the Bible, 2003).

- "There are in total **266.613.336 loyal angels of YHWH Echad** (*Cardinal Bishop* of Tusculum and Alphonso de Spina, **13th and 15th century**)." **This assumption restrict** the **numerical sum**, and so the **ministry assignments**, of the number of *Angels of YHWH Echad*, because there is an "**innumerable company of angels**" (see Heb. 12:22, KJV; *2nd Baruch* 56:14) **in the dimensions of heaven**, ministering to the heirs of salvation.

Pers. Rev. GR

Biblical Interaction with angels

Important:

- **Always worship God, not angels (Rev. 19:10, Col. 2:18,** *Ascen. Isaiah* 7:21), **but you can speak with them.**

- **Always test the spirits (1 John 4:1-3). Every angel wears on his breast a tablet inscribed with the name of YHWH (Rabbinic belief, own confirmation GR). Fallen angels can masquerading as an** *angel of light* **(2 Cor. 11:14,** *Apoc. Moses* 17:2, *Life of Adam and Eve* 1:9).

- **Clues to hierarchy of angels: found in Eph. 6:12, Col. 1:16, and 1 Cor. 15:24.**

- **Men don't become angels in heaven (Luke 20:36) (Jewish legends: Enoch transformed to** *Metatron***, Elijah transformed to** *Sandalphon***). In the** *Gosp. Nicod.* **and** *Apoc. Elijah* **Enoch and Elijah are the two witnesses of the** *book of Revelation***. "We are alive until the ends of time, to be comissioned by YHWH to resist the antichrist, be killed by him, resurrected after three days and to meet Yeshua in the clouds of His second coming."**

- **The name of an angel can be spelled differently (e.g.** *Uriel, Auriel,* **or** *Nuriel***); compare descriptions of function, appearance, test their words and actions, etc..**

- **The same spelling of a name can be a godly or fallen angel (Personal experience in my restoration process; fallen angel Raphael). Always test the spirits!**

- **Always ask God, Yeshua, to send angels for your specific need. He knows, what you need. Don't do it on your own, if you are not a mature trained discerning believer, even if you know names of angels or orders and their function in ministry (see book 2 of this series) to the saints.**

- **Angels of YHWH don't take any thanks, glory, or honor from saints for their ministry (happened to me sometimes, as I "said thanks" to the angel for his help); they always give it to YHWH Echad or Yeshua.**

- **Satan has created a copy/counterfeit of the heavens and has also copied the orders and functions of angels; after their fall angels execute the same functions under Satan.**

- **YHWH Echad is the great physician (Exodus 15:26) and He uses angels and/or worship music, colors, essential oils, etc., for healing and restoration of his people.**

- **In different translations of Apocrypha the names of angels mentioned in their interaction with mankind can vary (e.g. in** *1st Enoch* 10:2-3: *Uriel* **or** *Arsyalalyur* **bring the message of the coming flood to Noah). Compare context of the apocrypha, e.g. was the name of the angel used by the translator at other passages of this manuscript? Ask the Ruach HaKodesh for revelation and the right discernment!**

- **Even there is scriptural proof that angels of YHWH can bless men (Gen. 48:16) with words and hands layed or strechted out towards you, don't ask them for blessing you. Let them do this, when they have an assignment by YHWH Echad, or when they perform this from their own initiative. YHWH is the very first who blesses you (Numbers 6:24-27)!!!**

Order in the army of YHWH

God the **Father wills it**.

⬇

Yeshua the Word (the *living word* filled with *living water*, in [Gr.] "*zao*") **speaks it**.

⬇

The **Ruach HaKodesh brings it** to mankind.

⬇

Mankind **voices it** (born again sons and daughters). Speak words of faith; speak [Heb.] "*dabar*" also means "do YHWH Echad's business."

⬇

Angels **carry it out**

First-God the Father (*Elohim Avinu*).

⬇

Second-Yeshua the word.

⬇

Third-The Ruach HaKodesh, the liaison from Heaven.

⬇

Fourth-*Mankind*, God's under-ruler (born again sons and daughters).

⬇

Fifth-*Angels*, those excel in strength. "Do or act with effect, [Heb.] "*asah*," YHWH Echad's commandments."

Ps. 8:5: "For thou hast him (**man**, [GR]) made **a little lower** than **God** ([Heb.] "*Elohiyim*," NLT, Tanakh)."

Ref.: Dale M. Sides, Angels in the Army, 2004

PEACE BE UNTO YOU (Prayed in every synagogue at Shabbat celebration):

"**Peace unto you, you *ministering angels*, messengers of the Most High, the King of Kings, the Holy One, blessed is He. May your coming be in peace, messengers of peace. Bless me with peace, you messengers of peace. *Angels of the Most High*, blessed be He.**"

SHALOM AHLAYKHEM ([Heb.] original prayer to invite angels of YHWH Echad into Shabbat service):

"**Shalom ah-lay-khem mahl-ah-khay hah-shah-rayt mahl-ah-khay ehl-yom me-meh-lehkh mahl-khay hahm-lah-kheem hah-kah-dosh bah-rukh hoo bo-ah-khem l'shalom mahl-ah-khay hah-shalom malh-ah-khay ehl-yom me-meh-lehkh mahl-khay hahm-lah-kheem hah-kah-dosh bah-rukh hoo bah-r'khoo-ne l'shalom mah-l'khay hah-shalom mahl-ah-khay ehl-yom me-meh-lehkh mahl-khay hahm-lah-kheem hah-kah-dosh bah-rukh hoo tzay-t'khehm l'shalom mahl-ah-khay hah-shalom mahl-ah-khay ehl-yom me-meh-lehkh mahl-khay hahm-lah-kheem hah-kah-dosh bah-rukh hoo.**"

The heavenly, first estate of angels (Jude 1:6)

Levels/dimensions of Heaven: numbers?

3 (2 Cor. 12:2, *T. Levi* 2:6-12, and *Apoc. Paul* ch. 3), **5** (*3ʳᵈ Baruch* 11:1), **7** (oder **8**) (*Apoc. Abraham* 19:4-9, *T. Levi* 3:1-8, *Ascen. Isaiah* different verses, *Epist. Apostol.* **more** than **5**, *Gosp. Barthol.*, and *Apoc. Moses* 35:2), **9** (*Rev. of John* ch. 28), or **10** (*2ⁿᵈ Enoch* 22:1).

Ap. Ogbonnaya ("Dr. O"): based on Rev. 21:12-21

I. God/YHWH ("**Echad**," [Heb.] means: "*oneness-in-plurality*") Deut. 6:4, (no dimension of heaven),

II. **Trinitatis** dimension (Father, Son, Spirit), (no dimension of heaven),

III. The **divinity/human intersection dimension**, the embodiment of God in man (heaven of 6 dimensions) 1 Cor. 13:10, not reachable while on earth in human body,

IV. the **upper kingdom intersection** dimension, the sons of God (heaven of 12 dimensions) (12 apostles of the lamb level),

V. the **lower kingdom intersection** dimension, the sons of Israel (heaven of 12 dimensions) (12 tribes of Israel level).

Descriptions of the heavenly realms, the abode of angels:

*   **12 gates/portals in heaven** (Rev. 21:12-14), each **guarded by one of the 12 angels**: *Zehanpuryu, Atrugiel, Pathiel, Hadriel, Hadraniel, Kalmiya, Chamuel, Tradkiel, Uzial, Shoel, Tubuel*, and *Tsobiachel*. (Pers. Rev. GR; for angel names see later in this book or book 2). There is a "**secret password**" for **each gate** in the **lower dimensions** of **heaven** (*Ascen. Isaiah* 10:24). I (GR) got the revelation, that *speaking in tongues* articulate it, when **you should need it**.

*   27 **windows in heaven** (*Rev. Moses*, for *windows of heaven* see Mal. 3:10), each guarded by an angel (*gatekeeper-* or *pillar angels*)

*   **Different rooms** (each guarded by an angel; *gatekeeper-* or *pillar angels*): **Body parts room**, the **Library**, the **Treasury**, the **Hall of Faith**, **Storehouses**, **Wardrobe of Heaven** (Proph. Michael A. Danforth), etc.

*   **Angels**, after created by God **out of wind** and **fire** (see Heb. 1:7), **live in a place** in heaven, called "**City of angels**" (Proph. Brett Connell). It is like an **army camp** with **training** of angels, **manna houses, dwelling houses** (they differ between the different angels), **depots** with **supplies for angelic ministry** looking like a military airport (Proph. Michael van Vlymen), a **library, schools** to learn the 70 languages of the nations, an **oil press** for **producing essential oils** and a **depot** for the **healing balms of heaven**, etc.

*   **Archangels** have their **own houses** in heaven, **as have** the *Seven Spirits of the Lord* (see Isa. 11:2) (Proph. Kathy Madden)

Ref.: Ahmad Bruckman, Angels in Judaism, 2015; Alfred Edersheim, Jewish Angelology and Demonology, 2015; Andy Angel, Angels: Ancient Whispers of Another World, 2012; Erich Weidinger, Die Apokryphen, 2008; Adonijah Ogbonnaya, Hashamayim 1a, 2015; Brett Connell, Heavens Courts, 2016; Michael van Vlymen, Supernatural Transportation, 2016; Michael A. Danforth, Guardians of Spiritual Maturity, 2016

Ministry of angels vs. working of the Ruach HaKodesh

➢ The **Ruach HaKodesh** manifests the **nature** ("*Shekinah*") of **God**.

➢ **Angels** manifest the **intentions** of God. They **serve to do YHWH's pleasure** or **desire** ([Heb.] "*ratsown*").

➢ The **Ruach HaKodesh** brings the **Source of all life**.

➢ **Angels** bring according to what is **sovereign** or **what God has determined**.

➢ The **Ruach HaKodesh** brings the **Nature of God**.

➢ **Angels** are God's **agents of providence**.

➢ <u>Power of Angels:</u>   **Dependent on** and **received** from a source (**YHWH**).

It must be **exercised in accordance** with the **laws** of **material** and **spiritual world**.

Their **intervention** is **permitted** or **commanded by God** at His pleasure.

Ref.: Greg Crawford, Angels Helping Us Contend, 2013

➢ **Angelic preceptors/teachers**: In **OT times**, some Jewish leaders had **archangels as preceptors/teachers**, like: Adam-*Raziel*, Moses-*Tzaphkiel* and *Metatron*, and Abraham-*Tzadkiel* and *Yahoel* (a possible summary is shown in book 2). **In NT times**, the **Ruach HaKodesh** is our **teacher (John 14:26, Luke 12:12, and 1 Cor. 2:13)!** (for angel names see later in this book or book 2)

"**Angels** are the **executing body parts of God**, one minister says **of the Ruach HaKodesh**, e.g. His/**YHWH's** hands, feet, mouth (the **Executive**); **YHWH Echad** is the **Legislative**; we as the **body of Yeshua** are the **Judicature** (Proph. Nicole Sametat);" Ap. Robert Henderson says we are "*Judges*" of YHWH Echad (in his book: "*Prayers & Declarations that open the Courts of Heaven*, 2018").

Revelation of John ch. 50: "Then shall paradise be revealed; and the whole world and paradise shall be made one, and the **righteous shall be** on the **face of** all the **earth with my** (**Yeshua HaMashiach's** [GR]) *angels*, as the *Ruach HaKodesh* foretold through the prophet David (see Psalm 37:29):" "The righteous shall inherit the earth, and dwell therein for ever and ever."

Angels vs. Humans (I)

➢ **God's angels are**: supernatural, celestial beings of **pure spirit**. "They are **incorporeal spirits** (words of "*Michael*" about *angels* in *Testament of Abraham* [*T. Ab.*] 5:9), **with spirit bodies**." They are **mostly invisible** to prevent men from worshiping them.

➢ **Superior to humans** (without infilling of the Ruach HaKodesh) in: *wisdom*, *authority*, *holiness*, *power*, *goodness*, *beauty*, *intelligence*, and *abilities*; **perfectly obedient** ([Heb.] "*shama*") and **loyal** to God, they don't sin (loyal angels of YHWH). They **are not slack**; they are **not sleeping**.

➢ **Emotions** of angels of YHWH and fallen angels are **not impaired by sins** (loyal angels of YHWH don't sin!). Their **minds do not wander** like humans.

➢ The **presence of angels** generally brings a feeling of *acceptance*, **imparting**: *peace*, *joy*, and *patience* (Marie Chapian, Judith MacNutt) (see ministry of "*Malakhei Ha' Shalom*" [Heb.], in book 2 of this series).

➢ **Saints will "judge" angels in heaven** and **describe what is wrong** or **right** (1 Cor. 6:3).

➢ **Woman**, as **weaker vessel** (1 Pet. 3:7), **need spiritual covering** (authority and delegated authority over them) **as protection against the fallen angels**, especially the fallen *Irims*/watchers, see 1 Cor. 11:10: "For this cause ought the woman to **have authority on her head because of** the (fallen watcher, [GR]) **angels**." Fallen *Irims*/watchers try today to have sexual intercourse with woman again, as in the days of Noah or Lot (see Gen. ch. 6, Gen. 19:8, and Luke 17:26-28; appearing to woman as *Incubus* and/or *Succumbus spirits*).

➢ **There is no forgiveness of sins for fallen angels!** (**Jude 1:6**).

➢ **Saints will be totally transformed after their life in** the **image of Yeshua** (**2 Cor. 3:18**), having an **outward appearance** of the **splendor of angels** (*2nd Baruch* 51:5, *Ascen. Isaiah* 8:15).

➢ **The appearance of angels:**

• **Extremely white, light, bright, radiant, blue light** (= gold light); **transparent** or **clear** in God's presence (Proph. Ian Clayton). "Their **faces shine more than the sun**; Their **eyes shine like the morning star**. The **beauty** of their appearance **cannot be expressed**. Their **raiment is not woven**, but **white as that of the fuller** (*ethiop. Apoc. Peter*)."

• **Like stone, like crystal granite, like crystal**. Some look **like man**, some are **really tall** and **huge, or** some are **small** (more about the "*height*" of angels see **page 18**). **They often change their appearance according to their assignment! Some have no wings but have same body configuration as man** (Proph. Ian Clayton).

• For archangel *Michael's* **appearance** see *Jos. Asen.* 14:9: "**Face like lightning**, and his **eyes** were like the **light of the sun**, and the **hairs** of his **head** like **flames of fire** (*Michael* was angel "**in burning bush**" of Exodus 3:2, [GR]), and his **hands** and **feet** like **iron from** the **fire**." **Lightnings of glory fire** come **out of** His **hands** and **feet** (Pers. Rev. GR; for "*lightning countenance*" see Matt. 28:3, Mark 16:5, and Acts 1:10)."

Ref.: Marie Chapian, Angels in Our Lives, 2013; Judith MacNutt, Angels, 2012; Greg Crawford, Angels Helping Us Contend, 2013; Douglas Connelly, Angels Around Us, 1994; Dale M. Sides, Angels in the Army, 2004; Andy Angel, Angels: Ancient Whispers of Ancient Worlds, 2012

Angels vs. Humans (II)

Commonalities of angels and men:

1. They **have free will** and God-given capacity to choose their own destiny (2 Peter 2:4, Jude 1:6). Both **will be judged for their actions** (1 Cor. 6:3, 2 Cor. 5:10).

2. **Created to worship God** (Rev. 7:11, Phil. 3:3, Deut. 32:43, and *Supplement* to Daniel ch. 3 called *"Song of the Three"* [Septuagint]).

3. Are **under the authority of Yeshua HaMashiach** in the army of the Lord (Matt. 28:18).

4. Use **words as weapons of warfare** (Jude 1:9, Rev. 12:11) and **wear spiritual armor in battle** (Eph. 6:13-18, *T. Ab.* ch. 2). "**In heaven** there will be **excellency with** the **righteous surpassing that of** the angels (*2nd Baruch* 51:12)."

5. **War for supremacy of God's rulership** (Rev. 12:7, Eph. 6:12, *T. Moses* ch. 10).

6. Angels and men (should, my opinion [GR]) **celebrate the Shabbat** and **Shavuot** (*Book of Jubilees*, *Legends of the Jews*) and the **other biblical feasts** ([Heb.] *"moedim"*) **also** (Pers. Rev. GR). (1) "And **all *angels of the presence*** and *sanctification*, both great angelic orders, he (YHWH, [GR]) said, we should **celebrate Shabbat in heaven as it is on earth.**" (2) "...and that they (men, [GR]) **should celebrate Shabbat like us** (angels, [GR])...;" (3) "That's why it is **declared** and **recorded** on **heavenly scrolls/tables**, that **mankind should celebrate the Feast of Weeks** (Shavuot, [GR]) once a year for **renewal of their covenant; this feast is also celebrated in heaven** (for citations (1)-(3) see *Book of Jubilees* 2:17, 2:21, 6:18)." In Isa. 66:23 is mentioned, that "**at least**" at Yeshua's **1000 year reign** here **on earth all men will celebrate all** the *"moedim"* of Adonai!!!

7. They have a **distinct identity** and **personality**; their **name** is often a **clue to their function/destiny** (see name *"Gabriel"* in Dan. 8:16). There is importance of names in Judaism or other nations of the world (**not everybody** will **tell you his name**, to get a clue to their destiny, **fearing** you can **misuse his name** in **occult rituals**). **Men** will be **like angels in heaven** (see Matt. 22:30, *2nd Baruch* 51:10), that means **no reproduction**, e.g. children, **at all**.

8. Both are **limited in their knowledge** (two angels standing by Daniel asking a third angel, about the timing of future events, see Dan. 12:5-6). **The saints** must **increase in** the **knowledge of God** (see Col. 1:10).

9. They **are male** and **female** (female angels = *Shinarim* [Heb.], see **Zech. 5:9-11**: "...there came out **two women**, and **the wind was in their** *wings*..."). *Fallen* female angels are listed in the Bible, for example: Queen of Heaven (Jer. 7:18), Lilith (Isa. 34:14), or Diana (Acts 19:27). The *Seven-fold spirit of God* (Isa. 11:2): *Wisdom, Understanding, Counsel, Knowledge* (are *"female spirits,"* Proph. Ian Clayton). In deliverance ministry, I (GR) had encounters with many more **female fallen angels** from **Egyptian**, **Roman** or **Greek mythology**.

10. They can **bless people**, see **Gen. 48:16**: "The **angel** (*Michael*, [GR]) which redeemed me from all evil, **bless** the **lads** (the sons of Joseph, [GR])." (see also **page 24** and **page 49**)

Ref.: Marie Chapian, Angels in Our Lives, 2013; Judith MacNutt, Angels, 2012; Greg Crawford, Angels Helping Us Contend, 2013; Douglas Connelly, Angels Around Us, 1994; Dale M. Sides, Angels in the Army, 2004; Andy Angel, Angels: Ancient Whispers of Ancient Worlds, 2012

Characteristics of angels (I)

1. Have a **will** (Ps. 34:7) ("...the Angel of the Lord encampeth round about them that fear him, and delivereth them..."); are **intelligent** (Ex. 33:2, Heb. 2:2: "...if the word spoken through angels..."). **Played with *Behemoth*** (Job 40:14, [Septuagint], *before his fall* [GR]).

2. Have **emotions**, **joy**, can **weep** (for example *Yahoel* in *T. Ab.*, for more details see book 2), and **praise God** (Luke 2:14, Job 38:7, Luke 15:7, Luke 1:19, Ps. 148:2, *T. Ab.* 1:9, *Epist. Apostol.* ch. 51, and *PrMan.* 1:1) (angels dance, sing, and shout [GR]).

3. Are **curious** (*Epist. Apostol.* ch. 19, 1 Pet. 1:12) ("...which things [revelations, {Gr}] the angels desire to look into...").

4. Are **disciplined/obedient** (Luke 4:10, Ps. 103:20) ("...mighty ones who do His word..."). Angels **clearly hear YHWH Echad's words** and they **yield to them** (GR).

5. Are **patient** (Num. 22:22-35) ("...He would have killed Balaam, if it hadn't been for his donkey who spoke...").

6. Are **meek** (2 Pet. 2:11, Jude 1:9) ("...The Lord rebuke you..."); **stand in the fear of YHWH before His throne** (*2nd Esdras* 8:10). There are **myriads of angels**; they **cannot be counted** (Heb. 12:22, *2nd Baruch* 56:14, and *Ascen. Isaiah* 9:6).

7. Have **boundless energy** (Rev. 4:8) ("...They do not rest day and night saying..."); are **powerful** and **mighty** (Rev. 18:1). Have **highest activity** at the fourth night watch (from **3 a.m.- 6 a.m.**) (Ap. Bryan Meadows).

8. Angels **have a gender**: they are mostly male, e.g. *Gabriel* (male), *Lailah* (female); male angels are **circumcised at their creation** (*Book of Jubilees* 15:27). They **read** and **know the Torah**/written word of God (*Book of Jubilees*).

9. Angels are **restricted to one dimension** of heaven, **or are multidimensional** (Ap. Dr. O). **Archangels** are **multidimensional** (Pers. Rev. GR). Angels **work in the visible** and **invisible realms** (Numbers ch. 22, John ch. 20).

10. Angels **can appear as one unit**, a "*Legion*" (myriads in one); these units are **mostly warfare angels** (Ap. Dr. O).

11. Angels can **travel at inconceivable speeds** (Ezekiel ch. 1, Rev. 8:13, and Acts 8:39-40); **ascend into heaven** and **descend back to earth** (Gen. 28:12); **are holy** (Mark 8:38); **change** their **appearance between wind** and **fire** (*2nd Esdras* 8:11).

12. Angels in **human form** often appear as **young men** or **very handsome soldiers** (*T. Ab.* 2:2, 2:4-5).

13. Angels are being **taught wisdom by the Bride of Mashiach** [the **Ekklesia**, or the **Edah**] (Eph. 3:10, 1 Cor. 4:9).

14. Angels and archangels are **clothed with** the **mercy of YHWH Echad** as a **seal**. *Odes of Solomon* 4:6-8: "For who **shall put on Your** (YHWH, [GR]) **grace** and be rejected? Because **Your seal** (YHWH, [GR]) **is known**; and Your creatures are known to it. And **Your hosts** (angels, [GR]) **possess it**, and **the elect archangels are clothed with it**."

Ref.: Marie Chapian, Angels In Our Lives, 2013; Andy Angel, Angels: Ancient Whispers Of Another World, 2012; Adonijah Ogbonnaya, Hashamayim 1a, 2015; apostolic online teaching about angels, 2016

Characteristics of angels (II)

15. Angels are "**Elohim's appointed malachims** (as "*guardians*") **over the road of light, a way of instruction** and **authority**, e.g. **the narrow way, which leads unto life**" (*Epistel of Barnabas* 18:1, link to Matt. 7:13-14).

16. Angels **eat honeycomb/manna** (*Jos. Asen.* 16:9, here it is "*Michael*") or **pretend to eat unleavened bread** (Gen. 19:3). Manna is **white** as **snow**, full of **honey**, and **smells like myrrh** (*Jos. Asen.* 16:4-6). Manna is "angels food" (Ps. 78:23-25). "*Lechem Abirim*" [Heb.], is the **bread of the mighty** = (*Erelims*, [GR]) angels (Ps. 103:20). Angels **don't eat human foods**, because they are "*earthly* and *corruptible*" (speech by "*Michael*" in *T. Ab.* 4:10). **Manna tastes/transforms after/in that** what the **eater delights**, see *Wisdom of Solomon* 16:20-21: "Instead where of thou **feddest** thine own **people** with **angels food**, and didst send them from heaven bread prepared without their labour, able **to content** every **man's delight**, and **agreeing** to **every taste**." **Angels bread doesn't bring eternal life** (see John 6:49, 6:58)!

17. Special angels sit in the gates of heaven **witness** and **recording righteous deeds** of **saints** and **sinners** in scrolls, then after God get the scrolls, **he writes the deeds of the saint** in the *book of works/rewards* under the name of the saint (that is already written in, [GR]) (see *Apoc. of Zephania* 3:6-7) (**Recording Angels**, [Heb.] "*Adahim*," in depth study see book 2). **Salvation comes only through faith in accepting Yeshua (Rom. 3:24, 10:9-10)!!!** Rev. 20:15: "And whosoever was not found **written in the book of life** was cast into the lake of fire." (for the "*5 different recorded books in heaven*" see in depth study in book 2 of this series).

18. Angels **pray, intercede,** and **petiton** God on behalf of the saints **from their own initiative** in the **courts of heaven** and **council rooms of heaven, when they see/hear injustice** but they are **not our mediator, only Yeshua is it** (**1 Tim. 2:5**) (Pers. Rev. GR). **So don't pray to angels as your mediator, as the catholic church does! Example in *1st Enoch* for angelic intercession:** "*Michael, Uriel, Raphael,* and *Gabriel* looked from heaven and saw all the bloodshed on earth and all the injustice which was done and **they said together:**" "The voice of the screams of mankind fill the earth devoid of people and reach to the gates of heaven. The (deceased, [GR]) souls of men complain (about the Nephilim, [GR]) and they speak:" "**Bring this case (into the courts of heaven, [GR]) to the almighty God.**" "**Then spoke the four archangels to the Lord God Almighty.**" "...You see all this (iniquity, [GR]) and let the Nephilim do their evil work and don't say to us what we should do with them." In *Apoc. Moses* 35:2 **all angels petitoned** that **God** would forgive the **dying** Adam and let him be brought to *paradise* (*Eden*, [GR], graphic see **page 31**) in the *dimensions of heaven*, **not to Abraham's bossom in Sheol.** God replied: "I (YHWH) **promise** to thee (**Adam**) the **resurrection** (*Apoc. Moses* 41:2)." In *Gosp. Barth.* and *Gosp. Nikod.* is described the **resurrection** of **Adam by Yeshua**, as **Adam waited** for the Mashiach **in Abraham's bossom.**

19. Angels are **clothed with armors, robes, cloaks** (e.g. **for invisibility**) and **sashes** around their breasts. Sometimes I (GR) have seen angels with **breastplates with 12 gemstones** (e.g. with **12 rubies** or **12 sapphires**) **worn over their armors.** The **colors of clothes** thereof **differ** between the angels, depending on their **rank** or **function** (Pers. Rev. GR). Rev. 15:6: "And the seven angels came out of the temple, having the seven plagues, **clothed in pure** and **white linen**, and having **their breasts girded with golden sashes.**"

Ref.: Marie Chapian, Angels In Our Lives, 2013; Andy Angel, Angels: Ancient Whispers Of Another World, 2012

Characteristics of angels (III)

20. Angels **are not trees of** the **paradise!** (5 trees are known to the Jews (see *Writings of Philo*: *life, immortality, knowledge, apprehension, good* and *evil*). Angels **only acting as gardeners** (*gardener angels* see book 2 in this series), **helping God** to create the **first** (done at the **first creation of earth**, see "*Gap theory*;" more details see book 2) and **second garden** of Eden (Pers. Rev. GR). Here in *3rd Baruch* 4:8-11, the *second garden* is mentioned. "When God made the garden and commanded *Michael* to gather **two hundred thousand and three angels** so that they could plant the garden, *Michael* planted the **olive** and *Gabriel*, the **apple** (real fruit: **pomegranate**, Pers. Rev. GR); *Uriel*, the **nut** (real fruit: **dates**, Pers. Rev. GR); *Raphael*, the **melon** (real fruit: **figs**, Pers. Rev. GR); and *Samael*/later Satanael ("Poison of God," a "*Mavethim angel*," a fallen archangel described in more detail in book 2) the **vine** (they **planted** in *3rd Baruch* 4:8-11 **five** of the "*seven superfruits*" of **Israel**, only *barley* and *wheat*, **grass not trees**, are **missing** [GR])." "For at first his name in former times was *Samael*, and similarly **all the angels planted** the **various trees.**"

In the apocryphal "*Book of Giants*" **fallen watcher angels** are also planting a garden with **trees for idolatry** (worship of trees: Celtic religion performed by Druids, or other nature religions; "trees are worshiped as gods" or occult rituals are performed in "*evil forests*" [GR]). The fallen archangel Samael is according to "*Legends of the Jews*" **responsible for the drunkenness of Noah** (see Gen. 9:20) **through wine** and **the consequences/fruits** (here for Noah the **fruit** of **sexual immorality** [GR]; more informations about Samael see book 2).

The angel *Michael*, as "*gardener*," **learned Adam** how to **cultivate the earth, after they were thrown out of Eden** (*Life of Adam and Eve, Apoc. Moses*). "And Adam and Eve **searched** for nine days **for food**, like they had it, when they lived in Eden, but they **found nothing like** that, **only beasts** that **would give meat**. And **Adam spoke to Eve** saying, the Lord has given meat to the beasts of the field, but **we had the *angels food*,** e.g. *Manna* (GR)." Then **Satan** came and **decieved Adam** and **Eve** to **sin again through eating of meat** (this was **allowed by YHWH** the **first time after** the **flood**, see Gen. 9:3f.). Then **after Adam and Eve prayed**, YHWH sent *Malakim* and *Erelim* angels (GR) together **with *Michael*.** "And God, the Lord, sent *Michael* with different seeds that **he gave to Adam** and he showed him **how to cultivate the earth,** that it bring forth fruits, that **Adam** and **his descendants** can **live from the harvest** of the *fruits* and the *vegetation*." *Michael*, as "*angel of humanity*," **helped Adam** and **Eve**, after they were cast out of paradise, **to accomodate to life on earth** (*Apoc. Moses*). *Michael* was often sent by YHWH Echad to "**mentor**" and **teach Seth** (see *Apoc. Moses* 13:2, 43:1, 43:2), then *Michael* returned, thereby **worshiping Adonai**, to the **heavens.**

YHWH Echad placed **angels** as **guardians over trees,** the **highest specialized angel** is *Ilaniel* ("Tree of God"), an *Erelim*. *Ilaniel* is **dark green** in **color** and is a *Samayim* (this group of angels is described in more detail in book 2, Pers. Rev. GR).

21. There are "***Books of Angels***," Proph. Barbie Breathitt and Pers. Rev. GR, in which **all details about the names, hierarchy** and **function of angels are written.** These books are **protected by *guardian angels*** and are **stored** in a shelf **in the "*angelic courts of heaven*."** They are **available for usage,** when **angels are assigned for their ministry on earth.**

Ref.: Marie Chapian, Angels In Our Lives, 2013; Andy Angel, Angels: Ancient Whispers Of Another World, 2012

Five ways to cultivate a discerning spirit

1. Ask **YHWH Echad** for **discernment** (James 1:5, 1 Kings 3:9) and **to open our spiritual eyes** (Ephesians 1:18).

2. Seek **godly counsel** (Proverbs 11:14, Proverbs 15:22) to **sharpen your own skills**.

3. Stay **in the Word of YHWH Echad** (Hebrews 4:12, Romans 12:2). When we **know the word of YHWH Echad**, and **we know the character of YHWH Echad** by **studying His Word**, we will **cultivate discernment**. The **Ruach Elohim** and **the word agree** (1 John 5:8)!

4. **Exercise discernment** (Hebrews 5:11-14). **Test** by the **fruits** (Matthew 7:16).

5. Don't **go by what you see with the natural eyes alone** (John 7:24).

Other helpful questions to **test** whether **angels are from YHWH Echad or not**:

Are the angels **identified by non-biblical names**? Are the angels **given extrabiblical descriptions**? Are the angels **performing roles beyond** the **biblical picture**? Are the angels **sources of additional information beyond biblical affirmation**? Are the angels in any way **proclaiming another gospel**?

Prayer-**How do I guard against Deception**: from Barbara Wentroble (Freedom from Deception, 2008)

"Elohim Avinu, I pray for a passion for your word. Let the Bible be a lamp unto my feet and a light unto my path to keep me free from deception. Help me to study your Word and give me revelation. Empower me to test the spirits and know what is from you and what is from the evil one. I choose to reject anything that I do not have clarity on. As I follow You, I trust You to lead me into all truth. Thank you, HaShem, for helping me to guard against all deception. In Yeshua HaMashiach's name, Amen, Amen and Amen!"

Prayer-**Petition of Deliverance from Deception**: from Barbara Wentroble (Freedom from Deception, 2008)

"Elohim Avinu, I thank you that the plans You have for me are for good and not for evil. I thank you that you have revealed an area of deception in my life. I was blind but now I can see. I confess that I have been decieved and ask you to forgive me. Cleanse me from all unrighteousness. Give me a heart of humility and honesty. I want to be a lover of truth. I ask You to give me Your strategy that sets me free. I submit myself to your solution for my situation and submit myself to you. Thank you HaShem for directing my path and setting me free. In Yeshua HaMashiach's name, Amen, Amen and Amen!"

Ref.: Jennifer LeClaire, Angels on Assignment Again: God's Real Life Guardians at Work in the World today, 2017

Statements about angels (I)

- The archangel's ([Heb.] *"Rab Malakh"*) name is mentioned in **Jude 1:9**, **1 Thess. 4:16**, **Dan. 10:11-21** (Tanakh, Jewish Bible), and *2nd Esdras* 4:36. It is the **title** for the **head/administrator** of a group **of angels**. Is the **total number** of **archangels 7, 10** or **12**? I (GR) **believe** there are **more than 12** (for proof of my statement see later in this book and book 2). **Mostly** the **angels** whose **name is mentioned in scripture** (or **apocrypha**) are **archangels**. In *1st Enoch* 20:1-7 **seven archangels** are named: *Uriel, Raphael, Raguel, Michael, Sariel, Gabriel,* and *Remiel*. Archangels are also called *"glorious ones."* More about archangels see **page 23**.

- There is **scriptural proof** that **new angels could** be **created daily out of fire (Daniel 7:10)**, but **angels don't die daily** (see **Rev. 20:10**). Angels are *"ministers of fire"* (Heb. 1:7, *Gosp. Barth.*), or *"tongues of fire"* (Acts 2:3, Ap. Tim Sheets) or are *"made from the beginning, of flame and fire;" "the flames, change into spirits"* (*2nd Baruch* 21:6, 48:8).

- **Angels** are also **created from water, air** (e.g. **wind**, see Heb. 1:7), **fire, matter** (**not earth!**) **combined with** *spirit* (Ap. Dr. O.). **Air** and **fire** are **mentioned in Ps. 104:4**: "Who maketh his **angels spirits**; his ministers a **flaming fire**:" **Sometimes** angels are **combinations** of substances, therefore shining in **different appearances** (gold, diamond, glass) (Ap. Dr. O). *Legends of the Jews*: "When they (angels, [GR]) **descend** to earth, to **do** the **bidding** of God here below, either **they are changed from fire into wind**, or they **assume** the **guise** of **men**." "Angels are also called: *angels of the spirit of fire*, and the *angels of the spirits of the winds*" (*Rev. Moses*). Angels are **made by the breath of His** (YHWH's, [GR]) **mouth**. Ps. 33:6: "(and made, [GR]) *all the host* of them *by the breath of his* (YHWH's, [GR]) *mouth*."

- **Each nation has their designated godly angel prince** (but fallen *national* princes fighting against the godly ones); **70 nations = 70 princes** (see Gen. 10, *T. Naph.* 8-9). In *Legends of the Jews*: "**YHWH** and **His angels draw lots** with **names of the 70 nations**." Deut. 32:8: "When the Most High divided the nations, when He scattered the children of Adam, He **established the bounds of the nations** according to the **number of the angels** of God [Septuagint]." From these **70 nations** are **derived** all **other tribes** on the **earth** (GR).

- **All angels** (without the **7 angels of creation** and their **6000 ministering angels**, [see book 2 in this series]) **were created at** the **end of the first day** ([Heb.] *"erev"*) or the **beginning** (**1ˢᵗ night watch**) of the **second day of creation** (*Book of Jubilees, Legends of the Jews*). Angels were **classified** in (1) *angels of His presence* (see Isaiah 63:9, *Testament of the Twelve Patriarchs*; names of *angels of His presence* see **page 23**), (2) *angels of sanctification* or *angels of holiness* ("Kadishim" [Heb.]) (*Book of Jubilees, Legends of the Jews*, and *Dead Sea scroll* 1QM 7:6). *Kadishim* angels are mentioned in these three books as: *Phanuel, Michael, Metatron, Tzaphkiel,* and *Sariel*. Finally angels were classified in (3) *angels of nature* (*elemental spirits of the universe* in Col. 2:8, NIV), e.g. angels for **fire, wind, clouds, snow, ice, frost, hoar frost, hail, voices, thunder, lightning, heat, cold,** the **four seasons** (see *Book of Jubilees, 1st Enoch,* and *Rev. of John*).

- The angel *Michael* brought **earth** from the **4 ends of the earth** and **water** from the **4 rivers flowing out of Eden** (see **Gen. 2:10-14**, e.g. *Pison, Gihon, Tigris* and *Euphrat*) and **helped YHWH to create Adam** (*Gosp. Barth.*). **Angels helped YHWH** at the **creation of the earth** (see Job 41:24, [Septuagint]).

Pers. Rev. GR

Statements about angels (II)

- There are *guardian angels* (*Hadarim*) for every saint (Acts 12:7-10). See (1) Matt. 18:10: "**angels** watching over the little ones" (*shepherd angels*, see book 2 of this series); or (2) in *T. Jac.* 1:10 "**angels** visiting, *guarding*, strengthen Jacob in all things," or (3) in *1st Enoch* 100:5: "He (YHWH, [GR]) will set a *guard of the holy angels* over all the righteous and holy (saints, [GR])," or (4) in the book *Judith* 13:20: "As the Lord liveth, **His angel hath been my keeper**." Every saint has **one** *Hadarim*, **assigned 4 hours** after the **birth, staying** until his **death** (Proph. Pat Holloran). *Hadarim* **can complain** to **archangels** when **saints live in the flesh** (here parallel verses to Gal. 5:19) and **ask to resign** their **ministry assignment** (*3rd Baruch* 13:1-5; *Hadarim* appealing to "*Michael*" to "**transfer us** from them" {fleshly saints, [GR]}). **God** didn't **resign** their **ministry assignment**, but **removes** His **hand of blessings** and **protection** from fleshly saints **until they repent** (*3rd Baruch* 16:1-4). One **saint can have** so **much guardians as necessary**; Seer Kevin Basconi states: "Every believer in Mashiach has **at least one** angel assigned to their life and ministry." *Accompanying angels* "mostly" (Proph. Pat Holloran) *are not permanent, but temporary companions* (Rabbinic belief, Pers. Rev. GR). The *Personal Angel* remains at the **grave** of a deceased saint, **unless the family** of the **deceased one prays to YHWH Echad**, that **this angel** will be **used** again for the **protection of other** (**new born**, if they are there) **family members** or, **when** this is **not possible**, because **everybody** has a **personal angel**, yet, for the **protection of other humans** (Proph. Pat Holloran). Additionally there are "*familiar angels*" of family/generational lines (see **page 4**). *Hadarim* are **also associated to unbelievers**, but for them they perform **minimal protection duties until** they get **born-again**. (other details for *Hadarim* see in book 2).

- **Archangels** in the **throne room** can wear **crowns**, see *3rd Enoch*: "**he removes** his **princely crown**." "**Often these crowns** are as the *rainbow* in the *time of rain* (*3rd Enoch*)." "The **crowns** are **perfumed** with **spikenard** (*Apoc. Peter*)." **Archangels wear** their **crowns** only at "**special events**," like *special court sessions*, or the "*moedim*" of **Adonai** (Pers. Rev. GR).

- **Angels**, especially *personal* or *familiar* angels, **have the ability** *to* **transform into humans for max. 7 days** (Ap. Randy Demain) (**6 days?**, "**angels should work 6 days on the seventh is the Shabbat**" [*Book of Jubilees*]). **After this** time period they **become "earthbound,"** that's why they **were in hurry when destroying Sodom** and **Gomorrah** (Ap. Randy Demain, link to Gen. 18:22, Gen. 19:15). Even as *Raphael* spends more then **6 days with Tobit** on his journey, he (*Raphael*, [GR]) said, "**he was a** *vision* **not a human being**" (book *Tobit* 12:19).

- The **number of angels** in the **levels/dimensions of heaven**: "**100 myriads for every level/dimension** (*Gosp. Barth.*)." "**Archangels** have **496.000 myriads** of ministering **angels under them** (*3rd Enoch*)."

- **Every ekklesia/edah founded by God has two angels assigned to them!** (Prophets Ian Clayton, Pat Holloran). *Ascen. Isaiah* 3:15: "The *Edah of Yeshua* has **two assigned angels**."

- The **height of angels differs considerably**, see *Rev. Moses*: "The height of *Uriel* (approximately **5.6 km**) is **exceeded** only **by** the *Erelims*, by the *Irims*, **by** the angels *Af* and *Hemah* (more details about them see book 2), by the angel *Hadraniel* (**2.1 million miles tall**, more details about him in book 2) and of course by *Metatron* and *Sandalphon* (both angels are "*a 500 year foot journey tall*" [*Pesikta Rabbati* 20:3]) who are the **tallest angels** in the *dimensions of heaven*."

Pers. Rev. GR

Statements about angels (III)

- **Armies of heaven** ([Heb.] *"Mahanaim,"* link to Gen. 32:2): "There are twelve mazzalot [signs of the zodiac], each having thirty armies; each army, thirty camps [= castra]; each camp, thirty legions [compare Matt. 26:53]; each legion, thirty cohorts; each cohort, thirty corps; and each corps has 365.000 myriads of stars entrusted to it" (*Heb. Berach* 32b, [Alfred Edersheimer]). The **structure** of an **angel army** is **similar to** a **natural army** (Generals = archangels, officers, sergeants, and soldiers). I (GR), saw in the spirit **batches for** the **different angelic ranks**, like **soldiers** had them **to wear** in the **natural army**. **One archangel is associated** with **one zodiac**, but their **names are unknown to us** from the Bible, only from an apocrypha, the *Book of Raziel* (see book 2 of this series). Proph. Ian Clayton: "**Every tribe** of **Israel** had **its associated archangel** (also mentioned so in *Legends of the Jews*), they wrote His name on their shields." Only **4** (5 different names are mentioned in different translations of the scrolls) associated angels **are known, all others** (e.g. **8**) are from the *Book of Raziel* (see book 2 of this series). In the Dead Sea scroll *"War Rules of Israel,"* the following angels are mentioned: *Michael* and *Gabriel* in **front** of Israel's army; *Sariel* and *Raphael* [or *Raguel* alternatively for *Raphael*] at the **rear**. Based on my (GR) revelations is *Raguel* not associated with a tribe of Israel (see book 2). *Angelic protectors* of the **tribes**: *Gabriel* for Judah, *Michael* for Reuben, *Raphael* for Ephraim, *Uriel* for Dan. **22.000 ministering angels** (like 22.000 Levites in the camp of the Israelites) **per cycle** (3, 4 or max. 12 cycles in total) are **around** the *"Shekinah"* **presence** of God. There are **600.000 angels** in one **angel army** (*Legends of the Jews*). *Gabriel* always **went in front of Israel** see Ex. 33:2: "I will send an angel (*Gabriel*, [GR]) **before you**" and Num. 20:16: "sent an angel (*Gabriel*, [GR]), and has **brought us forth** out of Egypt."

- When **angels** get a **judicial assignment** from God, he **sends them out in two's** or **three's as** *witnesses* (for *biblical witnesses*: see Deut. 19:15, Matt. 18:16). Different examples for *judicial assignments*: In Gen. 18:2 you read about (1) YHWH/**Yeshua** with *Michael*, and *Gabriel* (as *"Beit Din"* [Heb.]) on the **way to Sodom** (*Michael* and *Gabriel* mentioned in *Legends of the Jews*, *T. Ab.* ch. 4 mentioned *"Michael"* only). (2) *Michael* with *Yahoel* **visit Abraham** to **bring him** after his death "**home**" (*T. Ab.*). (3) *Michael*, *Gabriel* and *Tzaphkiel* **cover Moses** after his death and **bring him to paradise**: "With God descended from heaven three angels, *Michael*, *Gabriel*, and *Tzaphkiel*. *Gabriel* arranged Moses' couch, *Michael* spread upon it a purple garment, and *Tzaphkiel* laid down a woolen pillow. God stationed Himself over Moses' head, *Michael* to his right, *Gabriel* to his left, and *Tzaphkiel* at his feet, whereupon God addressed Moses" (see *Legends of the Jews*). The book of Jude and *Ascen. Moses* mentioned only *"Michael"* at Moses funeral. **Otherwise one angel can be sent** (Luke 1:19, 1:26; (1) *Gabriel to* **Zachariah**, or (2) *Gabriel to* **Miriam**) or **more than three angels** are sent (see *Apoc. Moses* 40:2, 43:2) as *Michael*, *Gabriel*, *Raphael*, and *Uriel* prepare **Adam** and **Eve's bodies** for **burial**. "And there came the *three angels* (*Gabriel*, *Raphael*, and *Uriel* [GR]), together with *Michael*, and they buried her (Eve, [GR])."

- The **Heavenly Court-Bench of Three/** *"Beit Din"* **are**: Yeshua, *Michael*, and *Gabriel* (the *"Beit Din"* [Heb.] = *"House of the judge"* **record** of the **things spoken** in the **realm of the spirit**, see Matt. 12:36). *Michael* is associated with *Elohim Avinu* and *Gabriel* with the *Ruach HaKodesh* (Ap. Tim Sheets; *Ascen. Isaiah* 3:16 confirmed *Gabriel* as *the angel* of the Ruach HaKodesh). *Uriel* is now, after Lucifer's fall (teaching for "The Fall of mankind" see book 2), associated with or the *"personal angel"* of *Yeshua* (Pers. Rev. GR).

Angels and men at community of Qumran: a prototype for a NT ekklesia/edah

1. Had/formed a **special community**.

2. Had a **covenant** with God.

3. Had **special laws**.

4. Offered **bloodless sacrifices**.

5. Were to **live in perfect purity**.

6. **Not permitted** any **evil** or **sinfulness** in their midst.

7. **Praise** God, **worshiped** together, and **danced together** (Pers. Rev. GR).

8. **Possessed divine wisdom**.

9. As angels were tasked to **teach** other angels **things of God**, so **men** should teach each other **godly wisdom** and **godliness**.

10. Angels and men **go together to war**.

Ref.: Andy Angel, Angels: Ancient Whispers Of Another World, 2012

"**Now is a season when God is actively dispatching angels to assist you in a harvest you can hardly contain. So it is vital that we understand the role of angels, how to cooperate with their ministry**, and **how to avoid actions** and **words that hinder them** (Proph. Jennifer LeClaire, Releasing the Angels of Abundant Harvest, 2017)."

"**The Lord has been speaking about updates for His people. To actively work together with angels is the word for this season. You need in this season much needed insight into the angelic realm. Angels are assigned to bring forth blessing and breakthrough. One angelic encounter can shift your life!**" (Ap. Ryan LeStrange, in Releasing the Angels of Abundant Harvest, 2017)

"**In such a crucially important time in history of mankind, it is necessary to understand the role Angels of YHWH Echad will play in the days ahead!**" (Jennifer Le Claire, Angels on Assignment Again, 2017)

Angels and men co-laboring

1. By **answered prayers**

2. To **release supernatural provision**

3. To **release supernatural protection**

4. To **release supernatural revelation**

5. To **release the gifts of the Ruach HaKodesh** (1 Cor. 12:8-10; *healings, miracles, prophesy* etc.)

6. To **release decrees of YHWH's eternal word**

7. To **release supernatural signs** and **wonders (angels love to throw gold dust** or **other dusts of precious stones, like diamonds, on the saints** [Jeanie Jones, Signs and Wonders from God, 2016]).

8. To **rend** or **open the heavens over our lives** and **spheres of influence**

9. To **release supernatural salvation**

10. To **manifest the Mashiach's kingdom on earth as it is in heaven**

Ref.: Kevin Basconi, Angels: Miracles, Signs & Wonders, School of Angelic Ministry, 2015

"An **angel of prophetic awakening** (e.g. *Uriel*, [GR]) **has been sent into the body of the Mashiach to awaken new levels of prophetic giftings** (Ap. Robert Henderson, Unlocking destinies from the Courts of Heaven, 2016)."

"Angels are **released** and **activated by fragrances!** (Pers. Rev. GR)." Proph. Naomi Sheneberger (*Prophetic perfumer*) **created** through the revelation by the Ruach HaKodesh an **oil blend** called **"Jehovah Saboath Anointing Oil, Ps. 24"** that **activated and released** *warrior angels* **into spiritual battle.** See her shop ("*Rockroseministries;*" nsheneberger@yahoo.com) for purchasing this essential oil.

"**Now is a season** when **God**, after **verdicts in favor** of the **saints** or the **Edah are released, is dispatching angels** (*spoiler angels* of **YHWH Echad**, [Pers. Rev. GR and Proph. Nicole Sametat] more details see book 2) from the **courts of heaven** to **bring back** "*books of destinies from individuals, cities, regions,* and *nations*" **stolen by the enemy** (Ap. Robert Henderson, Prayers & Declarations that open the Courts of Heaven, 2018)."

Things that make angels angry or ground them

1. **Unbelief** or **words of unbelief**, **negative words**, **disagreement with YHWH's words**, **doubts**, **evil reports. Double-mindedness** in **prayer** ("even the **angels do not trust him**," *Apoc. Elijah* 1:26). "For double-minded" see link to Jas. 1:6-8 and Jas. 4:8.

2. **Not living in the covenant of YHWH, disobedience.**

3. **Saints living in the flesh; sin; religiosity binds** ([Heb.] *"deo"* = **throw into chains**) angels assigned to **assemblies, ekklesias/edahs, cities** and **nations** (Ap. Grant Mahoney, Moed Ministries, NZ).

4. **Disunity among brothers** and **sisters in the Mashiach.**

5. **Lies** and **deception, conniving** or **deceit.**

6. **Evil government rulings, laws, edicts.**

7. **Fear in spirit-filled believers, cowards, spirit of defeat.**

8. **To murmur, gripe, complain. Grieving Angels** (*Apoc. Sedrach* ch. XIV: "did **not hearken to** the **apostles/ministers** of YHWH or **to my word** in the Thorah, so they **grieve my** (YHWH's, [GR]), **angels**"). Similar passage "for grieving" see in Eph. 4:30.

9. **Evil decrees, negative proclamations.**

10. **Rebellion, witchcraft, idolatry, iniquity.**

11. **Lack of understanding (after repeated prophetic revelation); touching** or **taking YHWH Echad's Glory. Boasting** (*Apoc. Sedrach* ch. XIV: "**boast things** which I, (YHWH, [GR]) **do not accept, or my holy angels.**"). "For boasting" see link to Rom. 1:30.

12. **Passivity; not a doer of the word of YHWH, but a hearer only.**

13. **Fasting with wrong heart motive** ("whenever the **one who fasts** is **not pure** (wrong heart motive, [GR]) he has **angered** the **Lord** and **also** the **angels**;" *Apoc. Elijah* 1:18). See link to Matt. 6:16-18.

<u>Provoking angels results in</u>: **Sadness, barrenness, unfruitfulness, unprotectedness, hopelessness. This cancels angelic assignments, heard prayers are blocked, healings are blocked, provision is blocked, stopping angels to lead us in God's promise, with the result that promises are withheld** or **unfulfilled.**

<u>Scriptural proof:</u>

Job 5:1 [Septuagint]: "But (Job) call, if any one will hearken to thee, or **if thou shalt see any of the holy angels**" (because of your sin of not obeying God [GR]). **Speech of Eliphas to Job.**

Exodus 23:20ff: "Beware of the angel (here it is *Phanuel*, [GR]), and obey his voice, **provoke him not**; for **he will not pardon your transgressions**: for my name (in [Heb.] "EL," [GR]) is in him (inscribed, [GR])." More of *Phanuel* and *the meaning of his name* see **page 26.**

Ref.: Tim Sheets, Angel Armies, 2016; Pers. Rev. GR

Angels: their functions and ranks

> ➢ **Similar to gifts/ leadership functions of saints/ believers**:

1. *Functions all angels can principally do*, like **all believers can hear the voice of YHWH and prophecy**.

2. *Angels* with developed *special gifts*, like the **7 motivational gifts** (of **Elohim Avinu**, Rom. 12:6-8) or the **nine gifts** of the **spirit** (**Ruach HaKodesh**, 1 Cor. 12:8-10). When we **use our gifts, for YHWH's glory, they** can become a **spiritual mantle (permanent abitity to operate** in a **special gift); in our example** like **the gift of prophecy** (most teaching about *"special forces of angels"* see book 2 of this series and the *"12 orders of the Angels"* see **page 32ff.**).

3. *Angels* with *leadership function* (e.g. the *archangels* = the *glorious ones*, see Jude 1:8: "speak evil of the *glorious ones*"). **Archangels** are also *administrators*, like the **five fold ministry, ascension gifts** of **Yeshua**. In **our example** like the **office/ascension gift of the prophet** (more specific teaching about angels known by name see book 2 of this series).

A description of the *archangels* is found in *2nd Enoch* ch. 19:

"And thence those men (in white clothes, e.g. *angels* [GR]) took me (Enoch, [GR]) and bore me up on to the sixth heaven, and there I saw **seven bands (groups) of archangels,** *very bright* and *very glorious,* and *their faces shining more than the sun's shining, glistening,* and *there is no difference in their faces,* or *behaviour,* or *manner of dress*; and **these make the orders,** and learn the goings of the stars, and the alteration of the moon, or revolution of the sun, and the **good administration/government** of the world. And when they see evildoing they make commandments and instruction, and sweet and loud singing, and all different songs of praise. **These are the archangels who are above angels,** measure all life in heaven and on earth, and (**are above,** [GR]) **the angels** who are appointed over seasons and years, **the angels** who are over rivers and sea, and **the angels** who are over the fruits of the earth, and **the angels** who are over every grass, giving food to all, to every living thing, and **the angels** who write all of the souls of men, and all their deeds, and their lives before the Lord's face; in their (the *archangels,* [GR]) midst are six *Phoenixes* (YHWH's creation!, more details about them see book 2) and six *Cherubim* and six six-winged ones (*Chayot Ha Kodesh,* [GR]) continually singing with one voice, and it is not possible to describe their singing, and they rejoice before the Lord at his footstool."

• *Archangels* are **named** in the following chapters of *1st Enoch*: The **archangels of *1st Enoch* 40:9** (*Michael, Gabriel, Raphael,* and *Phanuel*) are: "angels of His Presence" (see Isa. 63:9, "*Malakhei Ha-Paniym,*" [Heb.]). "*Malakhei Ha-Paniym*" are also the **archangels,** **additionally mentioned** to the four listed above, in *1st Enoch* 20:1-7 (*Raguel, Sariel, Remiel,* and *Uriel*) (Pers. Rev. GR) plus *all the other archangels* mentioned in **different apocrypha** of the heavenly throne/courtroom **leading** an *angelic order* (*Metatron, Sandalphon, Haniel, Tzaphkiel, Tzadkiel,* and *Raziel*) (Pers. Rev. GR). "Now the **chief captains** of the **angels** are *Michael* (in *Ascen. Isaiah* 3:16: *Michael* is called "**chief** of the **holy angels**"), *Gabriel, Uriel,* and *Raphael* (*Epist. Apostol.* ch. 13)." As you read in this paragraph *Phanuel* or *Uriel* are **numbered** to the **four highest archangels** of YHWH Echad (GR).

Ministry of angels (*basic* functions all angels can do)

> ➤ **Angels are involved with the worship of God, executing the will of God, ministering to the heirs of salvation** and **Elohim Avinu/ Yeshua/ Ruach HaKodesh:**

1. **Physical protection**/protect **saints** (Ps. 34:7), **protection of the houses/rooms of the saints** (*2nd Esdras* 7:85, 7:95), **protecting the ekklesia/edah** (Rev. 1:20), **separate good from bad** (Matt. 13:49), **impart physical strength** to man in his **time of need** (Dan. 10:8-11, 16-19, Matt. 4:11, Mark 1:13, and Luke 22:43), and to **bring prayers of saints** as **bowls** of **incense before God** (Rev. 5:8, Rev. 8:3-4). **Inspire psalms** (*Gabriel* for some parts of the **book of Psalms** in "those **psalms which** have **not the name written**" [mentioned in *Ascen. Isaiah* 4:21]).

2. **Physical provision** (1 Kings 19:5), **watch over children** (Matt. 18:10), to **go before us** (Ex. 23:20), to **guide ministers** (Acts 8:26) and to **minister to saints** (Dan. 6:22).

3. **Encouragement** (Acts 27:23, Gen. 16:7-14), and to **strengthen us** (Luke 22:43).

4. **Direction** (Acts 8:26), **act as God's messengers** (Luke 1:19, 26), and to **impart God's will** (Acts 5:19). **Blessing** of (1) *saints* and (2) *people* (**Gen. 48:16** and Pers. Rev. GR). Read in *Jos. Asen.* 16:7: (1) "He (*Michael*, [GR]) **streched** his **hand out**, and **placed it** on her **head** and **said: You are blessed** *Aseneth...* ...and **blessed** too **are those** who **give** their **allegiance** to **YHWH** in **repentance**." and in *Jos. Asen.* 17:5: (2) "the *man* (*Michael*, [GR]) **blessed** them (seven yet **unsaved** virgins, [GR]) and **said:** YHWH, the Most High, will **bless you** for ever."

5. **Assist in answers to prayers** (Dan. 10:10), and to **drive spirit horses** (2 Kings 2:12).

6. **Carry believers home** (Luke 16:22), to **gather the elect** (1 Thess. 4:16), are **present in** the **Ekklesia/Edah** (Eph. 3:10), and **transportation of saints** (2 Kings 2:11, Ezekiel 8:3, Acts 8:39, and *Supplement* ch. 13, 14 to Dan. 2:35, 38). **Bringing godly prosperity**, including **divine connections/appointments** (Gen. 24:40), and to **enlighten** and **reveal** (Dan. 8:16).

7. **Return with Yeshua** (2 Thess. 1:7), **guard gates** (Gen. 3:24), **rule nations** (Dan. 10:13), **bind Satan** (Rev. 20:2), **regather Israel** (Matt. 24:31), and to **minister before God** (Rev. 8:2).

8. To **execute judgement** (Acts 12:23): Are then called *spirits of burning* (*torch angels* [GR]) and *spirits of judgement* (*bailiff angels, angels of death* and *destruction, hammer angels* and *avenger angels* [GR]). See **Isaiah 4:4** for names *"spirits of burning"* and *"spirits of judgement."* **Wage war in bodily combat** (Rev. 12:7), and to **know** and **assist** the **fulfilling of** the **destiny of saints** (Luke 1:13, Acts ch. 27). (for *judicial angel groups* see book 2).

9. To **give the laws** and **revelations** (Acts 7:53, Hebrews 2:2), to **witness confessions** (Luke 15:7), and to **accompany the Mashiach to earth** (Matt. 16:27).

10. To **exalt, worship,** and **glorify God** (Rev. 5:11, Ps. 97:7) In Ps. 97:7, **Tanakh**, stand here: "worship him (YHWH, [GR]) all [Heb.] *elohim*" = "**godly beings;**" an **angelic order** (see **page 32ff.**), **not** [Heb.] *"elohiyims"* = " **gods**"!

11. To **deliver from evil** (Matt. 25:41), and to **lead sinners to gospel workers** (Acts 10:3).

12. To **bring healing** (John 5:4), and to **appear in dreams** (Matt. 1:20-24).

Ref.: Greg Crawford, Angels Helping Us Contend, 2013; Judith MacNutt, Angels, 2012; Marie Chapian, Angels In Our Lives, 2013; Tim Sheets, Angel Armies, 2016

Comparison of angels and five fold ministry

Apostles-Archangels/Administrators

• **warriors** and **conquerors**, have strategic assignments, **oversee**, and direct others.

Prophets-*Malachim* (Messenger angels)

• have God's heart and intention, have **foreknowledge, bring a specific message**; bring message that may not be understood.

Pastors-*Irim* (Watcher angels)

• **watch over earth** and **humanity**, given **specific territory** message by YHWH, are **more resident**.

Teachers-*Cherubim*

• **proclaimers, protectors of truth** and God's **holiness**, protect what is precious to God.

Evangelists-*Seraphim*

• trying to **bring men into holiness of God**, look at how sin holds man back from approaching God. **Take coals of styrax** (e.g. *Liquidambar orientalis* **resin drops** [Anointing saints for *gracious speech*, speaking from a *gracious pure heart*, see Luke 6:45]) **from** the **incense altar in heaven to touch lips, heads**, and **hearts** of men.

➢ For me (GR), **archangels** are **not a specific order**, but a **rank** in the angelic hierarchy (see chapter "*12 orders of the Angels*" **page 32ff**. or **page 23**).

• Angels are **attracted especially to Apostles** and **Prophets** (the "*sent ones*") (Ap. Tim Sheets).

• During their **ordination in heaven** *five fold ministers* **receive mantles** with the **respective anointing for their ministry**. These spiritual **mantles**, or robes, also **have in the natural** an **anointing** like the **clothes** of the **Levites** in the **temple ministry**, see Ezekiel 44:19: "and they (the Levites, [GR]) **shall not sanctify the people with their garments**." (Pers. Rev. GR).

• **Apostles** and **Prophets set over** the **nations** by **YHWH Echad** are invited to the *council rooms* of **YHWH Echad** (Psalm 82), where **decisions concerning the whole earth are made**. (Pers. Rev. GR).

• The *heavenly angelic council* consists of the following *angels*: the **seven archangels** mentioned in *1st Enoch* 20:1-7: *Uriel, Raphael, Raguel, Michael, Sariel, Gabriel*, and *Remiel* **plus** the **three** other **archangels** *Zerachiel, Haniel*, and *Tzadkiel* (Pers. Rev. GR). *Regional/national angelic councils* consist of the *assigned territorial angels* of YHWH Echad and *angelic members* of the *heavenly angelic council*, together with *regional/national apostolic-prophetic councils*. They **release strategies** for **regional/national breakthrough** of the **kingdom of YHWH Echad**. (Pers. Rev. GR, Ap. Chuck Pierce ["now is the **establishment of** *new angelic councils* which will meet together with *apostolic-prophetic councils* to give *strategies for advancement*," in Barbara Wentroble, Accessing the Power of God, 2018]; for angel names see later in this book or book 2).

Ref.: Greg Crawford, Angels Helping Us Contend, 2013; Tim Sheets, Angel Armies, 2016

Angels of *Enoch* 40:9 and five fold ministry

Apostles-**Michael**: "Who is like God," *Benai Elohim* (Jude 1:9). He is merciful, long-suffering, a warring angel. *Michael* is **delegated prince angel/protector of Israel** (Dan. 12:1). An *angel of Shalom* (1st *Enoch* 40:8), protecting Shalom of Israel (in **Babylonia** the **life of Israel**, see *Baruch* 6:7). *Michael's* words about himself in *Jos. Asen.* 13:7-8: "I am the **commander** of the **Lord's house** and **chief captain** of **all the host** of the Most High:" He was clothed here "as a man **with a robe** and (having, [GR]) **a crown** and **a royal staff**." *Michael* has a **chariot of fire**, being **taken up** into **heaven** towards the east as he left Aseneth (*Jos. Asen.* 17:6). *Michael* is an *angel of deliverance* ([Heb.] "*Malakh Paltiylim,*" see 2nd *Macc.* 9:5) and *resurrection* ([Heb.] "*Malakh Qumim,*" see Luke 24:4; "*cumi*" or "*qumi*" see Mark 5:41). In *Cave of Treasures* is mentioned: "*Michael* then took away *Melchizedek*, when fifteen years of age, from his father Malach, and, after having *anointed him as priest*, as **commanded by YHWH Echad**, **brought him** to (*Jerusalem*, [GR]) the center of the earth, where **he served** at an **altar** standing **at the hill** (*Golgatha*, [GR])." *Michael* is also **mentioned** in **Rev. 17:1-7, 21:9** [Pers. Rev. GR].

Prophets-**Gabriel**: "Champion of God," or "Man of God," *Seraphim* (Luke 1:26). *Gabriel* has power over all *messenger angels*, and **brings intentions of God into hearts of men**. *Gabriel* has **foreknowledge** concerning God's intentions. *Gabriel* watches over the paradise and snakes. His symbols are a Shofar, carrying a lily, olive branch, or torch. *Gabriel* is the *angel of the power of God* (**YHWH**) and also the *angel of judgement* (see **1 Thess. 4:16**) and has been equated with thunder and majesty. *Gabriel* was the **angel** that **met Joseph** in the **field near Shechem** (Gen. 37:14, [GR]). Later *Gabriel* was **sent** by **YHWH Echad again** to speak **to Joseph** in Egypt and **to teach him all the languages of man** in that night (*Book of Jasher*).

Teachers/Pastor-**Raphael**: "God who heals," *Cherubim* (book *Tobit*). *Raphael* is the "*healing angel*" (body, soul, and spirit), who has **great love, happiness**, and **joy**. *Raphael* is the leader of the *healing angels*. *Raphael* is **instructing in healing processes** of saints and he **watches over the spirits of men**. *Raphael's* symbols are: a staff and sandals, a water gourd, and a wallet strapped over his shoulder, as well as a sword or an arrow that has been well sharpened. *Raphael* carries a **golden vial of healing balm** ("*Balm of Gilead,*" [GR], see Jer. 8:22). *Raphael* is an **angel of science** and an **angel of knowledge**. *Raphael* is "one of the *seven angels* standing in the **presence** of *YHWH*" (e.g. a "*Malakhei Ha-Paniym,*" e.g. *an archangel*; *Raphael's* **words** about *himself* in *Tobit* 12:15).

Evangelists-**Phanuel**: "The Face of God," *Seraphim*, (1st *Enoch*, 3rd *Baruch*). He has **oversight concerning repentance**. *Phanuel* is the **leader** of the *angels of repentance*, **bringing hope to those** who would **inherit eternal life**. *Phanuel* was the **angel helping Israel in the desert** (Pers. Rev. GR); for example see Ex. 14:19, 23:20, Zech. 12:8, and **Isaiah 63:9**: "In all their affliction He was afflicted, and the *angel of His presence* ([Heb.] "*Paniym*" = "*face* or *presence,*" e.g. *Phanuel*, [GR]) saved them." Queen **Esther** compared the **king Artaxerxes** of **Persia** to the **appearance** of *Phanuel* (Esther 5:2 [Septuagint]): "I saw thee, *my* lord, **as an angel of God**, thy *face is full of grace*." *Phanuel* is "the *archangel of penance*" and was said in *1st Enoch* to "**fend off devils** and **evil spirits**" that they may not "come before the Lord of spirits (YHWH, [GR]) to **accuse saints**" (in the **courts of heaven**, [GR]). *Phanuel* was mentioned in *3rd Baruch* 2:5: "**to show Baruch the dimensions of heaven** and **hell**." *Phanuel's* name is linked to Matt. 5:8: "Blessed are the **pure in heart**: for they shall **see God**."

Ref.: Greg Crawford, Angels Helping Us Contend, 2013; Justin Abraham, COBH-Angel Series, 2015; Tim Sheets, Angel Armies, 2016

Activating angels, loosing them (Matt. 16:19) (I)

"*Loosing angels*" ([Gr.] "*luo*") **means**: "**give angels liberty to perform their assignment** or **set angels free** (Proph. Jennifer LeClaire, Releasing the Angels of Abundant Harvest, 2017)."

➢ **Angels** are **activated through**:

1. *Our words* (Dan. 10:12), *speaking/singing with tongues of angels* (1 Cor. 13:1; own personal experience [GR]: After praying in *tongues of angels* I (GR) got protection from a little avalanche coming from the roof of my appartment house; it crushed near me to the concrete).

    Tongues of Angels: See (1) *Songs of the Sabbath Sacrifice*, (2) *Testament of Job* (in both books it is mentioned: "**angels sing praises** to God; **men** and **angels together praise God in tongues of angels**"), and (3) **Ps. 138:1**: "**I will sing psalms** to **thee before** the angels ([Heb.] "*elohim*")." In [Septuagint] is "*psalms*" translated as: "*singing in angelic tongues.*"

    Songs of the Sabbath Sacrifice (links to Psalms 38 and 92) contains **descriptions of worship of angels in Sabbath services**, the actual songs by angels are not mentioned. *Dead Sea scroll* 4Q401 (*Songs of the Sabbath Sacrifice*): "**They** (the angels, [GR]) **praise** the mysteries of His wondrous acts, a **voice of chants**, (they) can not (be silenced), God/YHWH makes mighty (deeds), **princes** of (His glory), they **proclaim secrete things**, at the issue of the lips of the King (of Kings) (e.g. Yeshua, [GR])."

    Testament of Job 11:24: "The **anointing** of the Ruach HaKodesh **felt like a garment/mantel**, **became a sash** (brought by *Beghedim angels* [GR]; *Beghedim angels* see book 2 of this series) **to her**." "and **she** (the daughter of Job, [GR]) **sang angelic hymns** in the **voice/tongues of angels**, and **she chanted** forth the **angelic praise** of God/YHWH while **dancing** (with a tambourine, [GR])." *Testament of Job* 11:28: "She **spoke** in the **dialect** of the *Cherubim*, **singing the praise** of the Ruler/HaShem (Yeshua HaMashiach, [GR]) of the cosmic powers (**Virtues/*Erelim***, [GR])."

    Tongues are **mentioned in OT**, too: From "**Hannah in** the **temple**" (see 1 Sam. 1:13, 15; Seer Adrian Beale: in his book "*The Mystic Seer*") and from the **prophet Isaiah** in an **OT apocrypha** the *Ascen. Isaiah* 6:10 "as he (**Isaiah** [GR]) was **speaking in the Ruach HaKodesh.**"

    As already stated at the "*Introduction of this book*:" "**Hebrew**, is the **speech of YHWH Echad** and the *angels* (see *Apoc. Paul* ch. 30)" and "the **language made use** of by **God** at the **creation of the world** (see *Legends of the Jews*)." There are **twelve angelic tongues/dialects** (Pers. Rev. GR).

2. *Winning the Lost* (Luke 15:10).

3. *Our worship* (especially **throne room** or **prophetic worship**); *Shofar* or *Silver trumpet* **sounds** (calling angels to war); *Banners* or *Flags* (movement of them); *Fragrances* (spiritual NT, see 2 Cor. 2:15; natural OT, see Exodus 30:7 [Heb.] "*Ketoret*" or *temple incense*). At the moment there is a **worldwide restoration** of the **usage** of "*Ketoret*" **in the Edah of Yeshua** and in the **personal worship times** with **YHWH Echad** (Pers. Rev. GR).

Ref.: Greg Crawford, Angels Helping Us Contend, 2013; Pers. Rev. GR

Activating angels, loosing them (Matt. 16:19) (II)

4. *Our declarations* (book of Daniel), *faith* (Pers. Rev. GR).

5. When we are *on assignment* from God (Acts 27:23; Paul as he went to Rome).

6. When *we are in rough situations* (Acts ch. 5, ch. 12; Ps. 34:7).

7. At the *time of* (our [GR]) *calling* (Exodus ch. 3, Acts 7:30).

8. When *we recieve doctrine* (Acts 7:38).

9. *During prayer* and *vision* (Acts 10:3).

10. *Giving* (*First fruits*, *Tenth*, *Offerings*, or *Alms* [especially to Israel/Jewish People, Pers. Rev. GR]). Biblical **example** of *"Giving* to activate angels" see Cornelius in **Acts 10:2-3** [G32: angel is here translated as *"Malachim"* in Strongs Concordance]. Here the angel *Tzadkiel* was **assigned** to Cornelius (Pers. Rev. GR). In the apocryphal book *Tobit* it was *"giving of alms"* (book *Tobit* 1:16) that **assigned** the angel *Raphael* to Tobit (book *Tobit* 3:16-17).

11. *Handsigns* (Ap. Dale M. Sides, in his book *"Angels In The Army"* [*"War rules of Israel"*]).

12. *Living* in *righteousness*, *holiness* and the *fear of the Lord* (Ps. 34:8, book *Tobit*).

Ref.: Greg Crawford, Angels Helping Us Contend, 2013; Pers. Rev. GR

Apostle John Mulinde in "Combat in the Heavenly Realms: How Satan stops prayers, MP3, 2000:"

"If one **who prays knows of the spiritual armor** and **is clothed with it**, the **answer comes by an angel who is also clothed in full armor. If one who prays don't care about being clothed in spiritual armor their angel comes to them without spiritual armor** (e.g. The *helmet of salvation* misses, when the praying person don't protect their thought life). Because of this fact **fallen angels clad in full satanic armor, empowered by ungodly sacrifices** and **prayers, can defeat the angels of YHWH Echad!** (*"defeat of YHWH's angels"* read more in book 2)."

Daniel Duval in "Prayers that shake Heaven and Earth, 2018" and Prophetess Ana Mendez Ferell, 2009:

"In Spiritual Warfare only the **angels of YHWH Echad** have the **ability to stop the attack** from **any human fragment** (spirit or soul fragment) or **ghosts** (coming out of the grave) or **astral projected spirits** that would attempt to bring sabotage, create havoc or ruination, including operating in collusion with the enemy (both known and unknown, seen and unseen). **Angels of YHWH Echad** can immediately **apprehend, isolate**, and put these **soul** or **spirit fragments to sleep** or **bring astral projected spirits** or **ghosts** before the **judgement seat of Yeshua HaMashiach**, if **commanded by YHWH Echad**."

The Angels of the *Shekinah* around YHWH Echad

In the Heavens: Throne of YHWH Echad   **On the earth**: The "*Shekinah*" of YHWH Echad

Behind YHWH

Raphael

N

Uriel

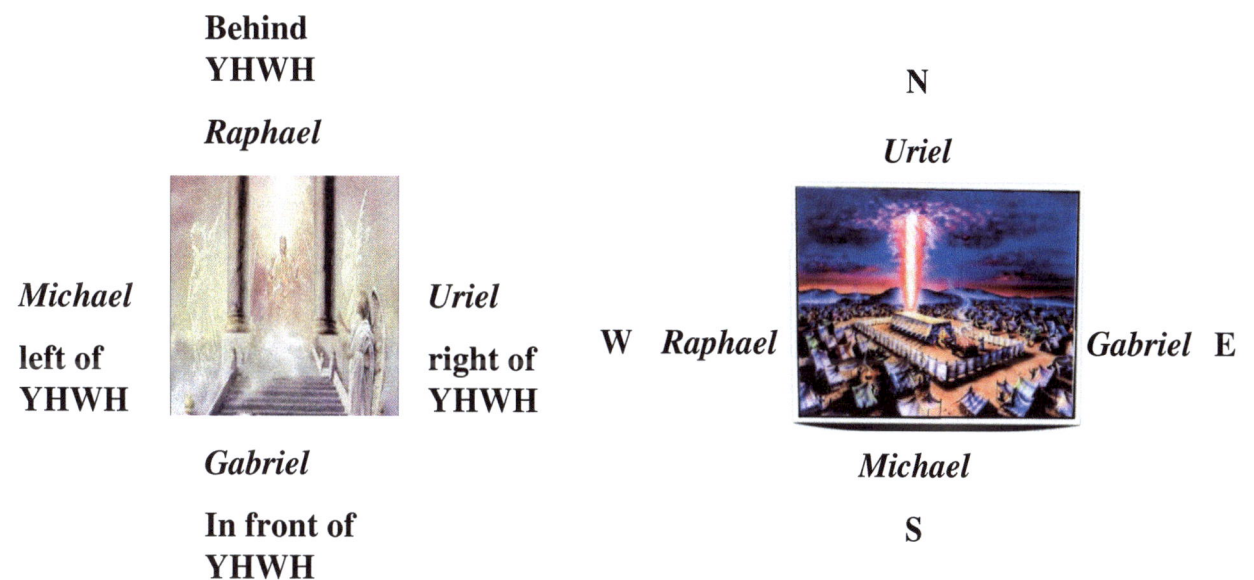

Michael

left of YHWH

Uriel

right of YHWH

W   *Raphael*

Gabriel   E

Gabriel

In front of YHWH

Michael

S

Ref.: Num. 2ff., *The War Rule* 1QM 9, *1ˢᵗ Enoch* 20:1-7, and *1ˢᵗ Enoch* 40:9

Pers. Rev. GR

Arts "*Throne room of heaven*" and "*Shekinah*" by unknown artists, both images are from public domain.

Why are *Seraphim* called *Seraphim*?

3ʳᵈ Enoch ch. 26: "Why are they, these angels, called *Seraphim*? Because **they burn** ([Heb.] "*saraph*") **the writing tables** of **Satan. Every day Satan** is **sitting, together** with his **highest leaders (fallen angels, in** a **satanic council room)** and **they write** the **iniquities of Israel on writing tables** which they **hand over to** the *Seraphim*, in order **that they** may **present them before the Holy One**, blessed be He, so that He may destroy Israel from the world. **But the *Seraphim* know** from the **secrets** of the Holy One, blessed be He, **that he desires not, that this people Israel should perish.** What do the *Seraphim*? **Every day** do they **receive (accept) them** from the **hand of Satan** and **burn them** in the **burning fire** over against the **high** and **exalted Throne in order** that they **may not come before the Holy One**, blessed be He, **at the time** when **he is sitting** upon the **Throne of Judgement, judging** the **whole world** in **truth**."

The battle order of Israel and angels around YHWH Echad

The battle order and "war rules for the nation of Israel" (**Numbers 2 ff.**, *The War Rule* **1QM 9**, *1st Enoch* **20:1-7**, and *1st Enoch* **40:9**)

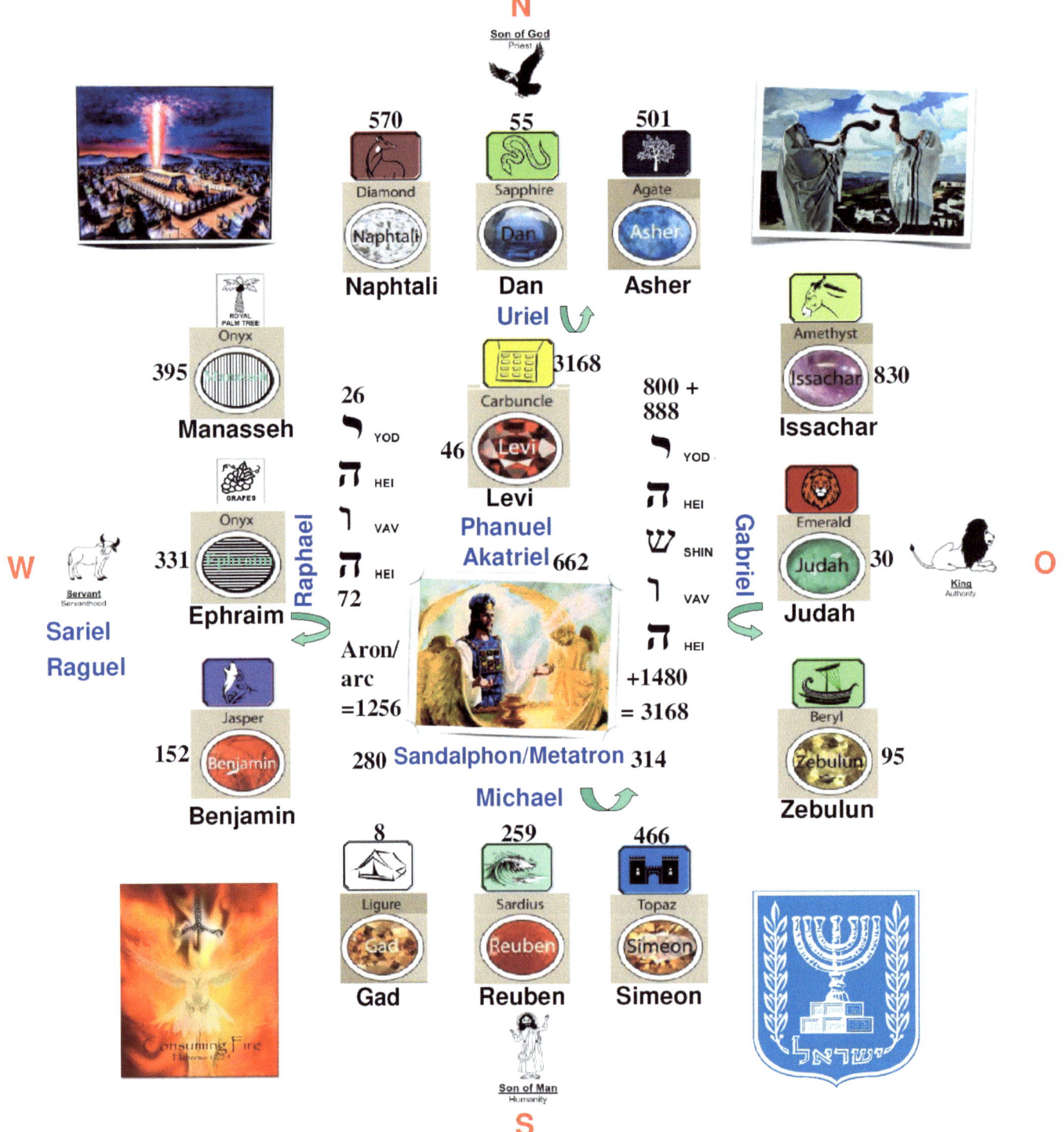

N

Son of God
Priest

570	55	501
Diamond	Sapphire	Agate
Naphtali	Dan	Asher
Naphtali	**Dan**	**Asher**

Uriel

Onyx
ROYAL PALM TREE
395 **Manasseh**

Amethyst
Issachar 830
Issachar

3168
Carbuncle
46 Levi
Levi

Phanuel
Akatriel 662

800 + 888

26 ᐟ YOD

ㄱ HEI

ㄱ VAV

ㄱ HEI

72

Aron/arc =1256

280 **Sandalphon/Metatron** 314

ᐟ YOD
ㄱ HEI
ש SHIN
ㄱ VAV
ㄱ HEI

+1480
= 3168

Gabriel

Emerald
Judah 30
Judah

King
Authority

O

Onyx
GRAPES
331 **Ephraim**

Raphael

Jasper
152 Benjamin
Benjamin

Servant
Servanthood

W

Sariel
Raguel

Beryl
Zebulun 95
Zebulun

Michael

8	259	466
Ligure	Sardius	Topaz
Gad	Reuben	Simeon
Gad	**Reuben**	**Simeon**

Son of Man
Humanity

S

Consuming Fire
Hebrews 12:2

Angel names are written in **blue color**; most single images are from *Jan Matthews* and *Rose Publishing*, the others are from public domain.

Ref.: Dale Sides, Angels In The Army (War rules of Israel), 2004; Perry Stone, Deciphering Endtime Prophetic Codes, 2015; Jan Matthews, Lively Stones, 2008; Rose Publishing, 12 Tribes of Israel, 2014, Pers. Rev. GR and graphic design by GR

Ten Orders of the Angels (Jewish Hierarchy)

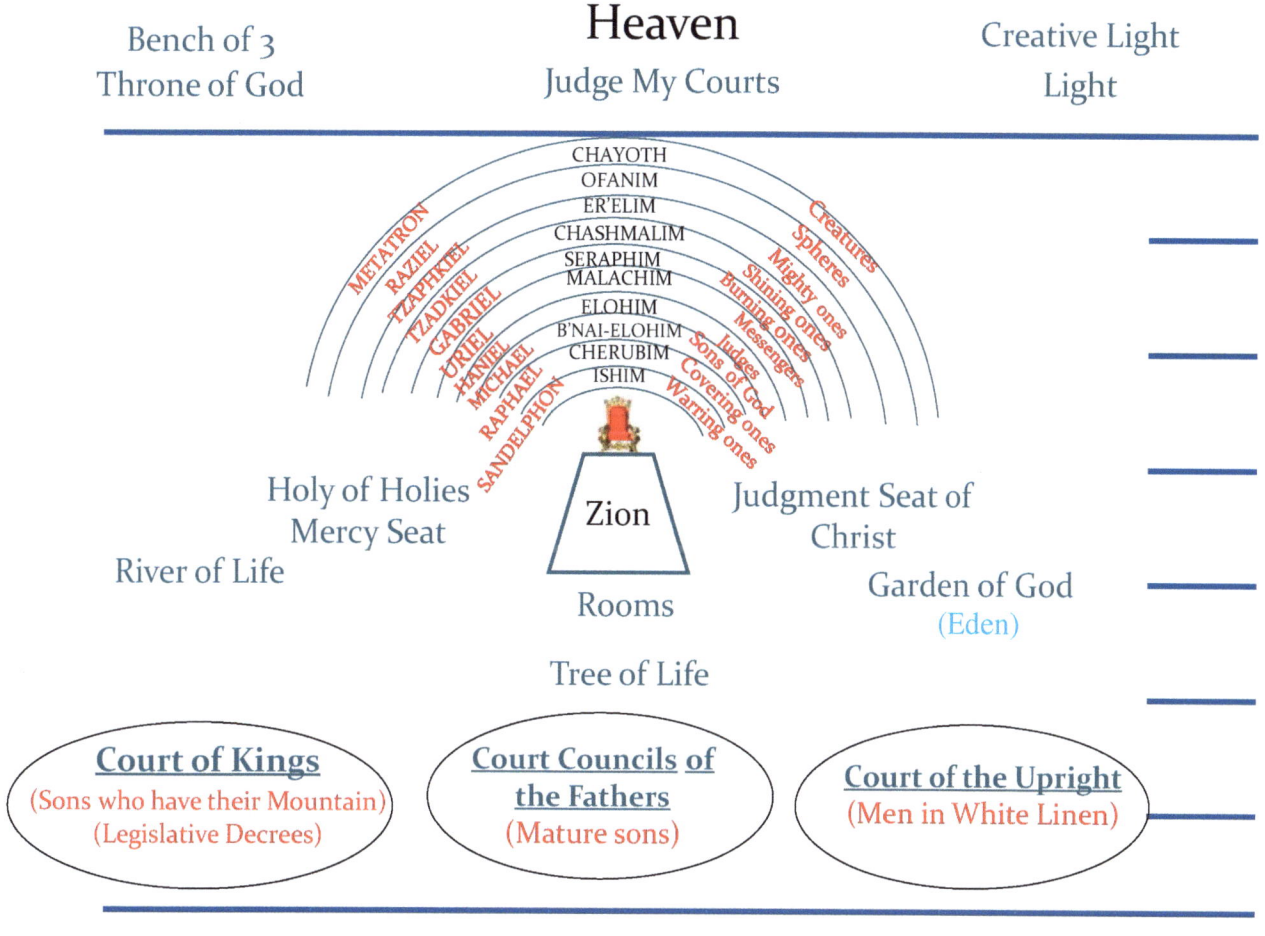

Ref.: Graphic by Ap. Mike Parsson, Freedom Apostolic Resources, UK, 2016. Teachings for this graphic by Seers Justin Abraham; Ian Clayton; Thomas Wright; Kathy Madden; and Grant Mahoney; all Pers. Rev. 2011-2015

The seven prophecies of *Uriel* to Ezra (*2nd Ezra* or *2nd Esdras*, [Septuagint])

Uriel reveals in *seven prophecies* the prophet Ezra **what will happen until everything is fulfilled (a new heaven** and **earth** [GR]) (parallel passages to the **book of Revelation**). First *Uriel* **appears in a vision, later even physically** in the presence of Ezra. For example in *2nd Esdras* 5:5 the **angel** *Uriel* **describes the days of the third trumpet**: "But if the most High grant thee to live, thou shalt see after the third trumpet that **the sun shall suddenly shine again in the night**, and the **moon thrice in the day**: And **blood shall drop out of wood**, and the **stone shall give his voice**, and the people shall be troubled." (parallel passage to *Epistel of Barnabas* 12:1, Rev. 14:9, and Rev. 16:4). In *2nd Esdras* 4:2 *Uriel* **admonishes** the Prophet **Ezra**, because **he didn't understand** why YHWH Echad allows **evil** to **be** in the **world**: "**Your understanding** has **utterly failed** regarding **this world**, and **do you think to comprehend** the **way of** the **Most High YHWH**?" (link to *1st Enoch* 99:10, and read Isa. 55:8-9). In *2nd Esdras* 4:36 *Uriel* speaks to Ezra about the end of the world: "(It is, [GR]) **when the number** of **those seeds** (e.g. **righteous men**, [GR]) like yourselves **is** (**ful-**, [GR]) **filled** (see **Matt. 13:38ff.**): for He (**YHWH Echad**, [GR]) **has weighed the age** in the **balance** (see **Daniel 5:27**; an *angel with a balance* in his hand *Soqedhodzi*, together with *Michael*, *Dokiel*, and *Zehanpuryu* as *angels of the balances* in the **courts of heaven**, see book 2 of this series)."

Twelve Orders of the Angels (Summary)

Rank	Angelic Class[1,]	Notes-Bible passages	Archangel[1,]
1	Chayot Ha Kodesh	"Holy Living Creatures" See Ezek. ch. 1 and 10.	Metatron
2	Ophanim	"Wheels" See Ezek. ch. 1 and 10.	Raziel
3	Erelim	"Mighty ones" See Isa. 33:7.	Tzaphkiel
4	Hashmallim	"Brilliant ones" See Ezek. 1:4.	Tzadkiel
5	Seraphim	"Six winged ones" See Isa. 6:2.	Gabriel
6	Malachim	"Messengers, Angels, Kings rulers" See Ps. 91:11; Job 1:14; 1 Sam. 16:19, 19:11, 14:20; and 2 Sam. 24:16; (angel 111x, messenger 98x in whole bible).	Uriel
7	Elohim	"Godly beings, Manlike ones" See Ps. 82:6, 8:5; Ex. 21:6, 22:8, and Ex. 22:9.	Haniel
8	Benai Elohim	"Sons of Godly beings, Sons of God" See Gen. 6:2; Job 1:6, 38:7; and Ps. 29:1.	Michael
9	Cherubim	"Covering ones" See Isa. 37:16; 2 Sam. 22:11; Ps. 18:10; and Gen. 3:24.	Raphael
10	Ishim	"Manlike beings, Princes of war" See Ps. 104:4; Gen. 18:2; and Dan. 10:5.	Sandalphon
11	Irim	"Watcher" See Dan. 4:13, 17, and Dan. 4:21.	now Uriel, former Semyaza
12	Zamarim	"Worshipping Spirits" See Rev. 5:11, Rev. 7:11; and Luke 2:13-14.	now Sandalphon, former Lucifer

Rank

Rank in hierarchy not known to me, GR

[1,] (Ap. and Proph. Thomas Wright; Ian Clayton; Kathy Madden; Dale M. Sides; Greg Crawford, and [Pers. Rev. GR])

Legends of the Jews: "The **most exalted in rank are those surrounding the Divine Throne on all sides**, to the **right**, to the **left**, in **front**, and **behind**, under the leadership of the archangels *Michael*, *Gabriel*, *Uriel*, and *Raphael*." "There are **ten ranks** or **degrees** among the angels."

The **last 2 ranks have been added by** GR, after prophetic revelation through the Ruach HaKodesh. The **number 12** represents **government** or **rulership of YHWH Echad** (GR).

Twelve Orders of the Angels (synergy) (I)

1. *Chayot Ha Kodesh*-Holy Living Creatures (Ezek. 1:15-21, *2nd Baruch* 51:11): **Metatron** ("One who serves behind the throne," or "One who occupies the throne next to the throne of glory"); is mentioned in *Enoch* (books 1-3), links to *"Lamentation"* [Septuagint]. Revelations below are Pers. Rev. GR, if not otherwise cited. *Metatron* keeps timing of everything/**administrate times** and **seasons** and is the **highest key keeper** for **spiritual doorways**. The *Key of David* (Isa. 22:22) is a **timeline**, you can **go in the glory realm back** and **forth in space** and **time**, bringing YHWH's prophetic promises or healings into the present time (Proph. Katie Souza, Proph. Bruce D. Allen). You often **get *Keys of David*** in **times of worship**. "When *Metatron* stands at the **door**/in the **gate** of the palace of YHWH, he **judges** all the **heavenly hosts**, (if necessary, [GR]), before YHWH (*Rev. Moses*)." *Metatron* is the **highest bailiff** in the **courtrooms of heaven, watching over** the **court protocol**. *Metatron* is one of the greatest (tallest) archangels/ "giant." *Metatron* is the scribe that sits beside the Godhead, who is under the Throne, and before it and who **watches over the ark** of the **covenant**. He is an *angel of Shalom*. *Metatron* **carries** the **prayers** of the **faithful** through the levels of heavens (see graphic about throne room on **page 31**) **onto** the **Godhead**, where *Selaphiel* ("Prayer of God," details see book 2) **present them as incense**. *Metatron* has a skin of flames, many eyes, 72 wings, and **fire inside**. *Metatron* **works** closely **together** with the angels *Seraphiel* ("Burning one of God") and *Jophiel* ("Beauty of God") (Pers. Rev. GR, more details for both angels see later in this book or book 2). **Moses** defeated **Jannes** and **Jambres** with the help of *Metatron* (see Gen. 5:24, 2 Tim. 3:8, and *Book of Jasher*, [Pers. Rev. GR]) and *Metatron* **rescued Moses** after his **murder** of the **Egyptian** (*Book of Jasher*, Exodus 2:12-15, [Pers. Rev. GR]).

Chayots **holding up God's throne** and **holding** the **"flat" earth** (biblical model of the earth based on the *books of Enoch*, see graphic in book 2) in its **proper position in space**. **Seers** of **HaShem** and **saints brought** to **heaven after their death**, but were **resurrected back to life**, have **seen** from **the dimensions of heaven, that** the **earth is flat** and **not round** (GR). *Chayots* **are known for their wisdom** and **revelation knowledge**. *Chayots* **keep silence** when the **Word proceeds out** of the mouth **of YHWH**, and **speak** when **He has ceased**. *Chayots* have a **fiery breath** when speaking (*Rev. Moses*). 4 *Chayots* are around the throne, they have **6 wings**. There are approximately **21 types** of *Chayots* with different functions (Proph. Ian Clayton). The **2 *cupbearer angels*** ([Heb.] *"Mashqehim angels"* or *"butler angels"*) of Yeshua (Seer M.R. Payne, 2015) are *Chayot Ha Kodesh* (Pers. Rev. GR). I (GR) meet them in the *"wine room of heaven"* (for *"wine room of heaven"* read teaching of Proph. Ian Clayton).

Another *Chayot Ha Kodesh* (Pers. Rev. GR), *Akatriel* ("The crown of God," more details of him see book 2) is mentioned in Rev. 21:15, Ezek. 40:3 and Zech. 2:1 (Pers. Rev. GR). Zech. 2:1: "I lifted up my eyes again, and looked, and behold a **man** (with **bronze appearance** [see Ezek. 40:3], e.g. an angel [GR]) with **a measuring line in his hand**." *Akatriel* is a *Middahim angel* (*"measuring angels,"* details see book 2). I (GR) met *Akatriel* at the sea of glas/trading floors in heaven with Melchisedek, having a **measuring rod** to **calculate** the **finances/prosperity given** to the **saints** after a **verdict in their favour** was going out **from** the **courts of heaven** (Pers. Rev. GR).

Ref.: Justin Abraham, COBH-Angel Series, 2015; Tudor Bismark, Prayer Summit, 2013; Hebrew internet source (archangel descriptions); Ahmad Bruckman, Angels in Judaism, 2015; Alfred Edersheim, Jewish Angelology and Demonology, 2015; Katie Souza, In the Midst, 2015; Bruce D Allen, Michael van Vlymen, Translation by Faith, 2016

Twelve Orders of the Angels (synergy) (II)

1. *Chayot Ha Kodesh*-Holy Living Creatures (Ezek. 1:15-21, *2nd Baruch* 51:11):

Other Holy Living Creatures are:

Hiel: ("Living of God"), ministering at the **throne room** of heaven as *butler angel*. His name is linked to Deut. 5:26: "For who is there of all flesh, that has <u>heard the voice of the living God</u> speaking out of the midst of the fire, as we have, and lived?"

Jathniel: ("Continued of God"), an *angel of prayer* and *intercession*. His name is linked to 1 Sam. 1:12: "And it came to pass, as <u>she continued praying before the LORD</u>."

Yomiel or **Jemuel**: ("Day of God"), ministering at the **throne room of heaven**, an *angel of times* and *seasons*, of the "*moedim*" of the Lord. His name is linked to Isaiah 13:6: "Wail you; for the <u>day of the LORD</u> is at hand;"

Jeriel: ("Throne of God"), ministering at the **throne room of heaven** as *butler angel* under *Akatriel*. His name is linked to Ps. 45:6: "<u>Your throne, O God</u>, is forever and ever: the sceptre of your kingdom is a righteous sceptre."

Joktheel: ("Veneration of God"), an *angel of prayer* and *intercession*. His name is linked to Ps. 99:9: "<u>Exalt</u> the LORD <u>our God</u>, and <u>worship</u> at his holy hill; for the LORD our God is holy."

Uiel: ("Wish and will of God"), an *angel of prayer* and *intercession*, ministering at the **throne room** of heaven. His name is linked to 1 Peter 2:15 and 1 Thess. 5:17-18: "<u>Pray</u> without ceasing. In everything <u>give thanks</u>: <u>for this is the will of God</u> in Yeshua HaMashiach concerning you."

Pathniel: ("Bread crumbs of God"); "*Path*" [Heb.] means: bits, bread, fragments, morsel, piece, piece of bread, pieces. *Pathniel* is **the highest specialized *Zikkaron* angel for bread of "*The Lord's supper*"** ([Heb.] "*Zikkaron*"), ministering at the **throne room** of heaven. His name is linked to Gen. 18:5: "and I will bring a <u>piece of bread</u>, that you may refresh yourselves; after that you may go on, since you have visited your servant."

Karmiel/Carmiel: ("God is my vineyard"); "*Karmel*" [Heb.] means: a planted field (garden, orchard, vineyard or park); by implication, garden produce: full (green) ears (of corn), fruitful field (place), plentiful (field). *Karmiel* is mentioned in the *Book of Raziel* and he is **the highest specialized *Zikkaron* angel for wine of "*The Lord's supper*"** ([Heb.] "*Zikkaron*"), ministering at the **throne room** of heaven. His name is linked to Isa. 5:3: "And now, O inhabitants of Jerusalem, and men of Judah, <u>judge</u>, I pray you, <u>between me and my vineyard</u>."

Ariuk: ("Preserver of Enoch") and **Mariuk**: ("Guardian of Enoch") (*Book of Enoch*), are **warrior** *Chayot Ha Kodesh* angels of the *Shekinah* **presence of YHWH Echad** and are **guardian angels** for **Enoch**, and additionally are *guardians of the earth* (see *Legends of the Jews*). In the Bibel there are **216 verses describing** the **shape of** the "biblical" **earth** (Nathan Roberts, The Doctrine of the Shape of the Earth, a comprehensive biblical perspective, 2017).

(all revelations to specific *Chayot Ha Kodesh* angels are Pers. Rev. GR).

Ref.: Justin Abraham, COBH-Angel Series, 2015; Tudor Bismark, Prayer Summit, 2013; Hebrew internet source (archangel descriptions); Ahmad Bruckman, Angels in Judaism, 2015; Alfred Edersheim, Jewish Angelology and Demonology, 2015

Twelve Orders of the Angels (synergy) (III)

2. _Ophanim_-Wheels (Ezek. 1:15-21): **Raziel** ("Secret[s]," or "Mysteries of God"); _Book of Enoch_. Revelations below are Pers. Rev. GR, if not otherwise cited. _Raziel_ is the personification of the "Divine Wisdom," he **protects/guards scrolls with recorded godly wisdom**, that are secrets of the universe (_Enoch_). _Raziel_ **stands** at the **very curtains** or **veil in heaven** (see graphic on **page 31**) **separating God from the rest of Creation** (_Enoch_). The curtains are open, e.g. angels open them, for blood-born, spirit-filled believers of Yeshua to enter, see Heb. 4:16, ch. 12. _Raziel_ was at **Horeb**, as **Moses got** the secrets of **Torah** from YHWH Echad (_Rev. Moses_, [Pers. Rev. GR]). He **hears** and **notes everything** that is **said** or **done** around the **throne of the Lord** (_Enoch_). _Raziel's_ **wings** are **spread out** to **keep off** the **fiery breath** of the _Holy Living Creatures_ from all other ministering angels (_Rev. Moses_). _Raziel_ **gives divine guidance** (_Enoch_). He was chief preceptor to **Adam**, who got a book (Torah, [GR]) from YHWH through _Raziel_ with recorded godly wisdom and knowledge to help him **live in righteousness, holiness** and **the fear of the Lord** (Pers. Rev. GR). _Raziel_ works closely together with the angels _Abdiel_ ("Servant of God," see **page 38**), _Lamiel_ ("His glory light comes from the ultimate source, the God of Israel"), or _Gamaliel_ ("Recompense," or "Reward of God") (Pers. Rev. GR, details for the last two angels see book 2).

**Wheels** **guarding God's throne in heaven**. They are **known for their wisdom**. _Wheels_ are very swift. Their color is beryl-like. _Wheels_ have **100 pairs of eyes** and **6 wings**. _Wheels_ are all **full of brightness, 72 sapphire stones are fixed** on their **right garments** and **72 sapphire stones are fixed** on their **left garments. 4 carbuncle stones** are **fixed** on the **crown of every Wheel**, the **splendor** of which **proceeds** in the four directions of the heavens. _Ophanims_ **move the throne of YHWH** and 4 _Ophanims_ are around the throne.

Other _Ophanims are_: **Ophaniel** ("God's wheel of the moon," an _angelic general_, more details see book 2). **Zehanpuryu** ("This one sets free, this one exempts," _3rd Enoch_), an _angel of His Presence_, is **one of the _highest gatekeepers_ of the grand palace** of YHWH and he **protects** angels and all other persons in the throne room of YHWH **from the fiery river issued** and **coming forth from** the **throne of God** (see Daniel 7:10). **Gallisur** ("Who reveals the reasons of the creator," _3rd Enoch, Rev. Moses_), is an angel, who, after YHWH allows him, **reveals** all the **secrets of the Torah** to the saints. **Chokmahel** ("Wisdom of God"), ("_Chokmah_" [Heb.] means: skill, wisdom, wisely, wits) is mentioned in 2 Sam. 14:20: "And my lord, (David, [GR]), is wise, according to the wisdom of an angel of God, (**Chokmahel**, [GR]), to know all things that are in the earth." _Chokmahel_ was the "_familiar, generational angel_" of the house of David (Pers. Rev. GR), serving David and his son Solomon and giving them **divine guidance through** the **wisdom of YHWH**. _Chokmahel_ works closely together with _Raziel_, is one of the highest _Ophanims_ and a **Sephiroth angel** (Pers. Rev. GR, details for **Sephiroth** angels see book 2). **Maowniel** ("Tabernacle of God"); "_Maown_" [Heb.] means: abode, of God (the tabernacle or the temple), den, dwelling,-place, habitation. His name is linked to Exodus 29:43: "And there I will meet with the children of Israel, and the tabernacle shall be sanctified by my glory." _Maowniel_ is an **_angel of godly secrets_** **ministering directly under** _Raziel_ and **ministering** at the **throne room** of heaven (Pers. Rev. GR).

Ref.: Justin Abraham, COBH-Angel Series, 2015; Tudor Bismark, Prayer Summit, 2013; Hebrew internet source (archangel descriptions); Ahmad Bruckman, Angels in Judaism, 2015; Alfred Edersheim, Jewish Angelology and Demonology, 2015

Twelve Orders of the Angels (synergy) (IV)

3. _Erelim_-Valiant ones/ Mighty ones/ _Thrones_ (Isa. 33:7): **Tzaphkiel** ("God's knowledge"); Books _Apoc. Moses_ and _Rev. Moses_. Revelations below are Pers. Rev. GR, if not otherwise cited. _Tzaphkiel_ **contemplates/focuses** about/**on** the **Godhead (Echad)** in all its glory. _Tzaphkiel_ is the **administrator** of the _throne angels_ (more details see book 2), that were **more powerful** and **mightier** than **all** the **other angels** (_Rev. Moses_, they are called _"special warrior angels"_ [GR]). _Tzaphkiel_ was the teacher of Moses, is an _angel of wisdom_ and loves to **teach** the **Torah** in **seventy languages** to the souls of men (the 70 nations of the earth, [GR]). He is an **instructor of young angels**, teaching them in the **school of angels** in heaven the seventy languages of men (link to the 70 nations on earth, [GR]). _Tzaphkiel_ is also an archangel/prince of the "Divine Presence," an _"angel of His presence."_ As **archangel** of the **Torah/written word** of **God** and **guardian angel of the Torah**, he is credited with having **taught Moses** the **name "YHWH"** and _Tzaphkiel_ is the _"angel with the horns/anointing horns of glory."_ _Tzaphkiel_ was also **assigned** by **YHWH** to **Noah,** guiding him in the **building** of the **ark** and helping to ensure the survival of his family. He **is also** the **highest guardian** of the **treasure rooms of Zion** (he **"smote** at evil treasurer **Heliodorus,"** see _2nd Macc._ 3:25; [Pers. Rev. GR]).

Erelims **"gets stuff done,"** they **administrate justice of heaven/courtrooms on earth with great rule** and **authority.** They are known for their courage and understanding. _Erelims_ have great love for men and watching over us most tenderly. The job of _Erelims_ is also to help us grow in holiness and **to avoid accidents** (**natural** and **spiritual**). _Erelims_ **bestow/impart, as servants of YHWH, God's grace** and **valor,** give encouragement and help a person to **survive hardship,** so that you **have a good end** as an overcomer. _Erelims_ have a special ability of **making miracles** (_"miracle angels"_). The **total number** of _Erelims_ is **estimated** to be **seventy thousand myriads of angels** made of **white fire** (mixture of fire and snow, see _Rev. Moses_), **some of them** are appointed over the grass, the trees, the fruits, and the grain (these angels are called: **"elemental spirits of the universe"** [Col. 2:8, NIV]). The **bodies** of _Erelims_ have **brilliant luminosity,** they **radiate spiritual perfection** and **emanate** the light of God with mirror-like **goodness.** _Erelims_ are humble. The **symbol** of _Erelims_ is a **throne.**

In _3rd Enoch_ the following _Erelims_ are described: _Oriphiel_ ("God is my neck"), is a _warrior angel_ (for _Oriphiel's_ name see 2 Sam. 22:41, Ps. 18:40), and a _guardian angel_ of the **planet Shabbatai.** _Yahriel_ ("Moon of God"), _is a guardian angel_ over the **moon**; _Baradiel_ ("Hail of God," is described in book 2) and _Barakiel_ ("Blessed by God," is described in book 2). _Cassiel_ ("Speed of God," _3rd Enoch_), an _Alahim,_ his **symbol** is a **hour glas,** is responsible for heavenly **translation** and **transportation** of saints, e.g. of **Philip** in Acts 8:39 (Pers. Rev. GR). _Cassiel_ "breaks open the heavens" and paves the way for "translation by faith" (Pers. Rev. GR). He is associated with **"space, time, and glory,"** an angel of **temperance** and the **vengeance** of **YHWH executing court verdicts** of **punishment** and **death** for ungodly leaders of the seven mountains of influence (Pers. Rev. GR). _Machidiel_ ("Fullness of God"), mentioned in _1st Enoch,_ is _watching over the almond trees_ and _almonds_ in the time period (90 days) around the _"moedim" Tu B' Shevat_ (Pers. Rev. GR). The almonds are the first _"first fruits"_ in Israel.

Ref.: Justin Abraham, COBH-Angel Series, 2015; Tudor Bismark, Prayer Summit, 2013; Hebrew internet source (archangel descriptions); Ahmad Bruckman, Angels in Judaism, 2015; Alfred Edersheim, Jewish Angelology and Demonology, 2015

Twelve Orders of the Angels (synergy) (V)

4. _Hashmallim_-Shining ones/ _Dominions_ (Ezek. 1:4): **Tzadkiel** ("Righteousness of God"). Revelations below are Pers. Rev. GR, if not otherwise cited. _Tzadkiel_ is often mentioned in scripture to be the _"angel of the Lord"_ ([Heb.] _"Malakh Elohim"_), as in e.g. Matt. 1:20: **"Fear not** to take unto you Miriam your wife" [Pers. Rev. GR]. _Tzadkiel_ was the angel **interacting** and **speaking with** the prophet **Zechariah**, see Zech. 1:9-5:11. For example in Zech. 1:12: "O LORD of hosts, how long will you not **have mercy** on Jerusalem and on the cities of Judah," [Pers. Rev. GR]. _Tzadkiel_ additionally **explained** to the **prophet Zechariah** all **his visions**, showing Him **all things to come** (Pers. Rev. GR). In **Gen. ch. 22** and the _Book of Jasher_ (Pers. Rev. GR) showed _Tzadkiel_ Abraham merciful kindness at **Moriah**. In Acts 10:3 brought _Tzadkiel_ **"salvation mercy"** for **Cornelius** (Pers. Rev. GR). The _angel of the Lord_ appears throughout the scriptures as the "help-mate" of the Trinity, in service to the Godhead and devotion to mankind. The _angel of the Lord_ **"brings"** Shalom (_angel of peace_), **freedom**, **benevolence**, **mercy** and **justice**. _Tzadkiel_ is a _chief warring angel_, attended by 496.000 myriads of ministering angels. _Tzadkiel's_ traditional _symbol_ is a _dagger_ (link to Gen. ch. 22) and a _staff_ (see Judges 6:20-24 for _Tzadkiel's_ **interaction** with **Gideon**, [Pers. Rev. GR]). The _Hashmallim_ angelic general **Lamiel** ("His glory light comes from the ultimate source, the God of Israel") is described in detail in book 2.

Dominions change color and **appear as cloud of color. They want** to be **around** the **glory displayed in your life. Every single color** of the **kingdom** (in total 7 colors, "rainbow" of God's glory; see books of Rev. and Ezek.) are **represented in them**. _Dominions_ **see glory color/spectra/light in you** (Col. 1:27). _Dominions_ are known for their **love, kindness**, and **grace**. They **ensure that** the **cosmos remains in order**. _Dominions_ **preside over nations**. _Dominions_ have **wielding orbs of light** fastened to the heads of their scepters or on the pommel of their swords. _Dominions_ focus on the details of the existence of the kingdom of God.

Other _Hashmallims_ are: _Jaasiel_ ("Made of God"), is a _warrior angel_, **guarding different levels of heaven**. His name is linked to Gen. 1:7: "And God made the firmament, and divided the waters which were under the firmament from the waters which were above the firmament: and it was so." _Jachdiel_ ("Unity of God"), is an _angel of mercy_ and _grace_, who **brings unity to the flock of YHWH**. His name is linked to Eph. 4:3: "Endeavoring to keep the unity of the Spirit in the bond of peace." _Jahliel_ ("Expectant of God"), is an _angel of mercy_ and _grace_. His name is linked to Ps. 62:5: "My soul, wait you only upon God; for my expectation is from him." _Magdiel_ ("Preciousness of God"), is an _angel of signs_, _wonders_ and _miracles_, **ministering under** the angel _Peliel_ ("Miracle," or "Wonder of God;" more details about him see book 2). _Magdiel's_ name is linked to Rev. 21:11: "Having the glory of God: and its radiance was like unto a stone most precious, even like a jasper stone, clear as crystal." _Pethuel_ ("Enlarged of God"), is an _angel of mercy_ and _grace for new seasons_, _cycles_ and _territories_. His name is linked to Exodus 34:24: "For I will cast out the nations before you, and enlarge your borders: neither shall any man desire your land, when you shall go up to appear before the LORD your God three times in the year." (all revelations to specific _Hashmallim_ angels are Pers. Rev. GR).

Ref.: Justin Abraham, COBH-Angel Series, 2015; Tudor Bismark, Prayer Summit, 2013; Hebrew internet source (archangel descriptions); Ahmad Bruckman, Angels in Judaism, 2015; Alfred Edersheim, Jewish Angelology and Demonology, 2015

Twelve Orders of the Angels (synergy) (VI)

5. _Seraphim_-Burning ones (Isaiah 6:2): **Gabriel.** (more details of him see **page 26**).

Revelations below are Pers. Rev. GR, if not otherwise cited. _Seraphims_ bringing holiness, bringing _fear of God_ with fire. They **burn holiness into your spiritual DNA.** _Seraphims_ **burn away iniquity, sins** and **transgressions of your life** and help Yeshua that **records of sin** are **removed.** _Seraphims_ **prepare you for service.** _Seraphims_ are known for their **work for justice.** _Seraphims_ burn eternally with **love** and **zeal for God**, with bright light. _Seraphims_ have **superior knowledge** of God. They **reflect God's goodness, His absolute holiness.** _Seraphims_ are the angels that are the **nearest to** the **heart of YHWH**, hearing and feeling His heartbeat of love for mankind or feeling His emotions. _Seraphims_ **singing music** of the **spheres/layers of heaven** (the "_Frequencies of creation_," see **page 6**, [GR]) and regulating the movement of the heavens. _Seraphims_ **proclaiming all day** and **night** in worship (called in [Gr.] "_Trisagion_" _prayer_): "Holy, holy, holy, is the LORD of hosts: the whole earth is full of his glory (Isaiah 6:2)." _Seraphims_ have **6 wings** and **four heads.**

One _Seraphim_ with a **head of an eagle** is called in _3rd Enoch_ "_Seraphiel_" ("Burning one of God," details see book 2). One _Seraphim_ (in the _Book of Raziel_) is called "_Abdiel_" ("Servant of God," jewish name mentioned in 1 Chron. 5:15). He is a _protector Seraphim_ and he **struck back**, **together with _Michael_**, with his mighty sword **the** co-conspirators/**fallen angels of Satan** from the boundary between Heaven and Sheol (link to Luke 10:18, John 12:31, Rev. 12:8-9, _Gosp. Barth._, and _Cave of Treasures_); forcing the fallen angels **into** the abyss. The angel _Jahaziel_ ("Beheld of God"), is an _angel of sanctification_. His name is linked to Ecclesiastes 8:17: "Then I beheld all the work of God." He **was the angel** of Isaiah 6:6-7, **purifying Isaiah for his ministry** (Pers. Rev. GR): "Then flew one of the _Seraphim_, (_Jahaziel_, [GR]), unto me, having a **live coal** in his hand, which he had taken with the tongs from off the altar: And he laid it upon my mouth, and said, Lo, this has touched your lips; and your **iniquity** is **taken away**, and your **sin purged**." One _Seraphim_ is called _Netsachiel_ ("Blood of God"). He is **one of the highest _angels of sanctification_** ministering **at the altar** in the **throne room of heaven** (Pers. Rev. GR). His name is linked to Heb. 9:14: "How much more shall the blood of Yeshua, who through the eternal Spirit offered himself without spot to God, **purge your conscience** from dead works to serve the living God?" Another **archangel** of the _Seraphims_, already mentioned on **page 26**, is _Phanuel_. In _3rd Baruch_ 10:1 it is written: "And when I (Baruch, [GR]) had **learnt all these things from** the **archangel** (_Phanuel_, [GR]), he **took** and **led me into a fourth heaven**." _Phanuel_ is "the **interpreter** of the **revelations to those** who pass **through life virtuously**" (_3rd Baruch_ 11:8, speech by _Michael_ about _Phanuel_). _Phanuel_ **speaks to Noah** after the **flood about planting a vineyard**. _3rd Baruch_ 4:12ff.: "And I, (_Phanuel_, [GR]), **came** and **spake to him** (Noah, [GR]) **the things concerning it**" (whether God would allow Noah to use a vineyard for cultivation or not, [GR]). Then **God sends** the angel _Sariel_ ("Prince of God," or "Command of God;" details for him see book 2) **to Noah**, to **speak about** the **mystery of** the **vine**. _Phanuel_ is the angel of "_The Shepherd of Hermas_," too. He is in this apocrypha described "as a **man glorious in appearance, dressed like a shepherd**, with a **white skin wrapped around him** and with a **bag on his shoulders** and a **staff in his hand**." He is called "_the angel of repentance_" here.

Ref.: Justin Abraham, COBH-Angel Series, 2015; Tudor Bismark, Prayer Summit, 2013; Hebrew internet source (archangel descriptions); Ahmad Bruckman, Angels in Judaism, 2015; Alfred Edersheim, Jewish Angelology and Demonology, 2015

Twelve Orders of the Angels (synergy) (VII)

6. *Malachim*-Messengers (Ps. 91:11): **Uriel** ("God is my Light," or "Flame of God"), *Book of Enoch*. Revelations below are Pers. Rev. GR, if not otherwise cited. *Uriel* has scars on his body, is tall, has 2 swords in his hands, and a scroll in his bag. *Uriel* is also leader of the *Irim angels*. *Uriel* **brings** the **announcement of Simsons birth** to his parents, **ascending in** the **flame of** the **altar to heaven** (Judges 13:6, 20, [Pers. Rev. GR]). *Uriel* also **announces the judgement** of **Rev. 19:17** (Pers. Rev. GR): "And I saw an angel, (*Uriel*, [GR]), standing in the sun; and he **cried** with a **loud voice**, saying to all the fowls that fly in midheaven: Come and gather yourselves together unto the supper of the great God." *Uriel* also unveils seven **prophecies to** the prophet **Ezra** (mentioned in *2nd Esdras*, see **page 31**). *Uriel* is also the **angel** of **Rev. 14:6** and **Rev. 14:18** (Pers. Rev. GR) (called *"the angel who had power over fire"*) and *Uriel* was **responsible** for the **hail destroying** the **barley harvest** of **Egypt** (see Exodus 9:23, [Pers. Rev. GR]). *Uriel* also **leads a** *special group of worship angels*, the *Shachakim* ([Heb.] "refiners") see *Legends of the Jews* ch. 4 and *Rev. Moses*: "In the **second heaven** Moses saw the angel *Uriel*, standing three hundred parasangs (approximately **5.6 km tall** or **high**), with **his army of fifty myriads** (= 500.000) of *Shachakim, Shahakim, Shachaim* or *Shahavim* ("Sha'avah" in [Heb.] means: "tempest" or "rushing storm") *angels* (diff. spelling of diff. translations), all **fashioned out of water** and **fire**, and all **keeping their faces turned toward the** "*Shekinah*" while they **sang a song of praise** to YHWH Echad" (more details see **page 47**). "*Metatron* explained to Moses, that these were the **angels** set over the **clouds**, the **winds**, and the **rains**, who **return speedily**, as soon **as they have executed the will** of their Creator (YHWH Echad, [GR]), **to** their station in **the second of the heavens**, there **to proclaim the praise** of YHWH Echad." In some translations of *1st Enoch* 10:2-3 it is written, that *Uriel* was sent by YHWH Echad to **warn Noah** about the **upcoming** *Great Flood* (my revelation to this passage read in book 2): "Then said the Most High, the Holy and Great one spoke, and sent *Uriel* to the son of Lamech, and said to him: "**Go to Noah** and tell him in my name "**Hide thyself!**" and reveal to him **the end that is approaching**: that the whole earth will be destroyed, and a **deluge** is about to **come upon** the **whole earth**, and will **destroy it**." After **judgement verdicts** from the **courts of heaven** have been **brought on** the **Nephilim** and the **fallen watchers** including their two main leaders Semyaza and Azazel, *Uriel* **discusses their fates**: "And *Uriel* said to me (Enoch, [GR]):" "Here shall stand the **angels who have connected themselves with woman**, and **their spirits assuming many different forms** are **defiling mankind** and shall **lead them astray** into **sacrificing to fallen angels** and **demons** as gods." "Here shall they stand, till **the day of** the **great judgement in** which they **shall be judged** till they are made an end of. And the **women also of the angels** who went astray **become sirens** (demon possessed beautiful woman, [GR])." Additionally in other apocryphas it is written: (1) That *Uriel*, through **checking** the **doors** of **Egypt for** the **lamb's blood during** the **plaque**, was the angel who **recorded on scrolls which houses were protected by** the **blood** of the **lamb** from the **death** brought through the *angel of death* and *destruction Ezrael* ("Help of God," details see book 2). (2) That *Uriel* **holds** the **key to the** "*Abyss*" (link to *Apoc. Peter*), and (3) that *Uriel* **led Abraham** on his **journey** to the **west** as "**he got out of** his **country**, from his kindred, and **from** his **father's house** (see Gen. 12:1)."

Ref.: Justin Abraham, COBH-Angel Series, 2015; Tudor Bismark, Prayer Summit, 2013; Hebrew internet source (archangel descriptions); Ahmad Bruckman, Angels in Judaism, 2015; Alfred Edersheim, Jewish Angelology and Demonology, 2015

Twelve Orders of the Angels (synergy) (VIII)

6. *Malachim*-Messengers (Ps. 91:11):

Revelations below are Pers. Rev. GR, if not otherwise cited. *Malachims* **bring justice/judgement of God to** the **face of** the **earth from** the **galactic council of God**. *Malachims* are also called **rulers of the *King of Kings*** (Yeshua, [GR]) and they are known for their beauty and mercy. *Malachims* are **responsible for communication** within the ranks of heaven, and they are known for being outgoing and talkative. Language poses no barrier for *Malachims* (they speak the seventy languages of the 70 nations of the earth, [Pers. Rev. GR]). *Malachims* **are skilled at drawing others** (saints and sinners) **into dreams** and **visions** (sinners have only dreams, Prophets Beale and Thompson, in book *"Divinity Code"*).

One of the highest *Malachim* angels responsible for **divine dreams** and **visions** is the angel *Haziel* ("Vision of God"). He is the **angel** of **Gen. 31:11 speaking to Israel** and **giving him in a dream wisdom** for getting his inheritance from Laban (Pers. Rev. GR). Gen. 31:11f.: "And the **angel of God**, (*Haziel*, [GR]) **spoke unto me in a dream**, saying, Jacob: And I said, Here am I. And he said, Lift up now your eyes, and see, all the rams which leap upon the cattle are striped, speckled, and spotted: for **I have seen all that Laban does unto you.**"

Zophiel ("God's spy") is a *bailiff angel*, an *Adahim*, a *Quaraim* and a *covenant angel* (more details about the different angel groups see book 2). He **watches** that the **covenant with YHWH Echad** and **all its regulations are held by Israel or** the **saints**, that's why **he is send out to earth from** the **courts of heaven** or the **council rooms of YHWH Echad** (Pers. Rev. GR). *Zophiel* also is a *guardian angel* of the **planet Shabbatai** and he **helped Noah to build the ark** (*Rev. Moses*). *Zophiel* **helped Noah's family to survive** the **flood** (*Rev. Moses*) and *Zophiel* **is the angel** of **Judges 5:23 which proclaimed** the **curse of YHWH Echad over Meroz** (Pers. Rev. GR): "**Curse you Meroz**, said the **angel of the LORD** (*Zophiel*, [GR]), **Curse you** bitterly **the inhabitants thereof**; because they **came not to the help of the LORD, to the help of the LORD against the mighty.**"

The angel *Azbugah* ("Garment of God," or "Girdle of God"), is mentioned in *3rd Enoch*. He is an angel, who **knows the mystery of God's throne of glory** and **clothes resurrected saints** in the **4 pieces of garments of Yeshua** (see Isa. 61:10: "**2 robes of salvation, 1 robe** of **righteousness** and the **white bridal garment.**" [Pers. Rev. GR]). The **first three garments** are **given at our salvation** to **cover** our **spiritual nakedness** and to **restore** the **glory of righteousness**, the **white bridal garnment** is **given to us in heaven** (see Rev. 19:8). *Azbugah* was the **angel** of **2 Kings 1:3, 15** bringing **Elijah a ministry assignment** from YHWH **to go** and **confront king Ahaziah** (Pers. Rev. GR). 2 Kings 1:15: "And he (Elijah, [GR]) arose, and went down with him (*Azbugah*, [GR]) unto the king." *Azbugah* is the **leader** of the *Beghedim* angels (details see book 2).

Ref.: Justin Abraham, COBH-Angel Series, 2015; Tudor Bismark, Prayer Summit, 2013; Hebrew internet source (archangel descriptions); Ahmad Bruckman, Angels in Judaism, 2015; Alfred Edersheim, Jewish Angelology and Demonology, 2015

"**Angels are not perfect**, if this would be the case Lucifer had not sinned and was cast out from the heavens. **Even if angels are spirit beings created with the fire** and **glory of YHWH Echad**, there is **only one which is perfect** in **every aspect** and that is the God of Israel, **YHWH Echad** (Proph. Nicole Sametat)."

Twelve Orders of the Angels (synergy) (IX)

7. _Elohim_-Godly beings (Ps. 82:6): **Haniel** ("Joy of God"). Revelations below are Pers. Rev. GR, if not otherwise cited. _Haniel_ is mentioned in _3ʳᵈ Enoch_ 6:1-18: "_Metatron_, the Angel, the Prince of the Presence, said to me:" "When the Holy One, blessed be He, desired to lift you (Enoch, [GR]) up on high, He first sent _Haniel_, the Prince, and **he took you** (Enoch, [GR]) from their midst in their sight and **carried you in great glory** upon a **fiery chariot** with **fiery horses**, servants of (YHWH's, [GR]) glory" (see Gen. 5:24, _Book of Jasher_). _Haniel_ guards the gates of the West Wind, watches for heat coming out of the West and protects against the satanic gatekeeper of the bottomless pit (Apollyon/Abbadon, [GR]; see Rev. 9:11). _Haniel_ is an _angel of Shalom_. _Haniel_ **holds** the **keys** to the **palaces of heaven** and **allows people** into **various heavenly places after God calls them up.** _Haniel_ is an _Alahim angel_ (details see book 2) and a _guardian angel_ of the "tree of life."

Elohims have **human form** and are the **size of humans**, that's why they are also called "Look like man angels." _Elohims_ look like us and they are known for their commitment to the victory of good over evil. _Elohims_ are **administrators** of the **kingdom realm** of the **angelic world** and **they also bring justice/judgement from God.** In the **Bible** are mentioned visitations of men with angels in human form: In **Acts 12:15** the question arose "**whether Peter** or **his angel is there,**" or see **Heb. 13:2** "some have unaware entertained angels." I (GR) believe, that especially _personal_ or _familiar angels_ appear in **human form** to the saints, because of personal testimonies I (GR) heard or experiences I (GR) myself had.

The angel _Remiel_ ("Mercy of God," or "God's exaltation"), is the **2ⁿᵈ in rank** of the _**Elohim**_ **angels** (Pers. Rev. GR). _Remiel_ tells the prophet Baruch in _Apoc. Baruch_ or _2ⁿᵈ Baruch_ 71:3: "I have come to tell you these things, because **your prayer has been heard with the Most High.**" Then _Remiel_ gives Baruch "**a vision** of the **hope** that he says **will come to the world** when the **Mashiach brings its sinful, fallen state to an end** and **restores it** to the way **God originally intended it to be:**" "And it shall come to pass, when he (Yeshua, [GR]) has brought low everything that is in the world, and has **sat down in peace** for the **age** on the **throne of his kingdom**, that **joy** shall then **be revealed**, and **rest shall appear**. And then **healing** shall **descend in dew**, and **disease shall withdraw**, and **anxiety** and **anguish** and **lamentation pass from among men**, and **gladness proceed** through the **whole earth**. And **no one** shall again **die untimely**, nor shall **any adversity suddenly befall**. And **judgments**, and **abusive talk**, and **contentions**, and **revenges**, and **blood**, and **passions**, and **envy**, and **hatred**, and whatsoever things are like these **shall go into condemnation** when **they are removed**," (_2ⁿᵈ Baruch_ 73:1-4). _Remiel_ showed **Baruch heaven** and **hell**: "the **multitude of innumerable angels**, the **flaming hosts**, the **splendor of** the **lightnings**, the **voice** of the **thunders**, the **hierarchy of** the **archangels**" (_2ⁿᵈ Baruch_ ch. 59). _Remiel_ **defeated the army of Sennacherib**, see 2 Chron. ch. 32, Isaiah 37:36, _1ˢᵗ Macc._ 7:41, _2ⁿᵈ Macc._ 15:21, _Sirach_ 48:2, and _2ⁿᵈ Baruch_ 63:6: "And thereupon the **Mighty One** commanded _**Remiel**_ His angel who speaks with you (Baruch, [GR]) and he went forth and **destroyed their multitude.**" _Apoc. of Zephania_ 6:12: "**His** (_Remiel's_, [GR]) **face** is **shining in glory**, he (_Remiel_, [GR]) **is girded** with **a golden girdle, his** (_Remiel's_, [GR]) **feet like bronze** (Pers. Rev. GR)."

Ref.: Justin Abraham, COBH-Angel Series, 2015; Tudor Bismark, Prayer Summit, 2013; Hebrew internet source (archangel descriptions); Ahmad Bruckman, Angels in Judaism, 2015; Alfred Edersheim, Jewish Angelology and Demonology, 2015

8. _Benai Elohim-Sons of God/ Powers (Ps. 29:1):_ **Michael**; he is a tall angel and a warrior. Revelations below are Pers. Rev. GR, if not otherwise cited. In _6ᵗʰ Baruch_ or _Letter of Jeremiah_ it is written about _Michael_: "For my angel, (_Michael_, [GR]) is with you (Israel, [GR]), he will **watch over your** (Israels, [GR]) **life**" or alternatively translated "**your** (Israels, [GR]) **lives will be in his care.**" (more details of _Michael_ see **page 26**)

Benai Elohims **hold your throne** in the **spiritual realm, until** you are **mature enough to sit in your mountain** and **rule as a king** ("the _throne, garments,_ and _crown_ of saints," see _Ascen. Isaiah 7:22_ and _Apoc. Elijah 1:8-10_). _Benai Elohims_ are **involved with** the **angelic court of God**. _Benai Elohims_ focus their work on **giving glory to God**. _Benai Elohims_ are **bearers of conscience** and keepers of history. _Benai Elohims_ are **angels of death**, **birth**, **resurrection** and _deliverance_. _Benai Elohims_ are concerned with ideology, philosophy, theology, religions on earth and **scrolls associated with these things**. _Benai Elohims_ are advisers and policy planers, but **intervene only after** they got a mandate/**assignment from God**. _Benai Elohims_ **assist men in overcoming temptation**. Their colors are green and gold and **they carry a flaming sword**. _Benai Elohims_ **help** individuals in their struggles **against evil thoughts**.

One of the highest _Benai Elohims_, a warrior angel, an _angel of deliverance_ is the angel **Hofniel** ("Fighter of God," details see book 2). **Adbiel** ("Disciplined of God"), is an _avenger angel_. His name is linked to Job 36:10: "He opens also their ear to discipline, and commands that they return from iniquity," (more details about him see book 2). Other _Benai Elohims_ are: **Meshezabiel** ("Delivered of God"), is an _angel of deliverance_. His name is linked to Exodus 10:9: "Blessed be the LORD, who has delivered you out of the hand of the Egyptians, and out of the hand of Pharaoh, who has delivered the people from under the hand of the Egyptians." **Pagiel** ("Accident of God"), interpreted by GR as "Prevent accidents through God's grace in prayer and intercession," is an _angel of deliverance, punishment, prayer_ and _intercession_. [Heb.] "_Paga_" means: to impinge, by accident or violence, or figuratively by importunity: cause to entreat, fall upon, make intercession, intercessor, intreat, lay, light upon, meet together, pray, reach, run. _Pagiel's_ name is linked to Ezra 9:13: "And after all that is come upon us for our evil deeds, and for our great trespass, seeing that you our God has punished us less than our iniquities deserve, and has given us such deliverance as this." **Putiel** ("Contempt of God"), is an _angel of punishment_. His name is linked to Job 12:21: "He pours contempt upon princes, and weakens the strength of the mighty." **Shubael** ("Captives returned by God"), is an _angel of deliverance_. His name is linked to Ezek. 39:25: "Therefore thus says the Lord GOD; Now will I bring again the captives of Jacob, and have mercy upon the whole house of Israel, and will be jealous for my holy name." **Yadiel** ("Hand of God"), is an _angel of punishment_. He was the **angel** of **Acts 13:11**: "And now, behold, the hand of the Lord, (**Yadiel**, [GR]), is upon you, and you shall be blind, not seeing the sun for a time. And immediately there fell on him a mist and a darkness; and he went about seeking some to lead him by the hand." _Yadiel's_ name is linked to Exodus 16:3, 9:3: "Behold, the hand of the LORD is upon your cattle which are in the field." _Yadiel_ was **the angel of the fifth plague**, killing the cattle of the Egyptians (for _Yadiel_ see also Job 19:21, 23:2, and Ezek. 8:1). (all revelations to specific _Benai Elohim_ angels are Pers. Rev. GR).

Ref.: Justin Abraham, COBH-Angel Series, 2015; Tudor Bismark, Prayer Summit, 2013; Hebrew internet source (archangel descriptions); Ahmad Bruckman, Angels in Judaism, 2015; Alfred Edersheim, Jewish Angelology and Demonology, 2015

Twelve Orders of the Angels (synergy) (XI)

9. _Cherubim_-To be near (Gen. 3:24): **Raphael**; He is a tall angel. (more details of him see **page 26**).

Revelations below are Pers. Rev. GR, if not otherwise cited. _Cherubims_ are **covering ones** and bring **revelation of** the **knowledge of God**. _Cherubims_ have a **breastplate** with **9 stones**, the **three missing stones** are from the tribes Gad, Asher, and Issachar = _overcoming power, yield royal seed/life_, and a _servant living for others_. 4 _Cherubims_ are around the throne. _Cherubims_ **interact with men** through **worship, during** their **3 times "Holy" proclamation** (like Isaiah 6:2). _Cherubims_ are gold in color and they are **known for** their **work to help people** in a **worship/glory atmosphere to deal** with **sin that separates** them **from God**. _Cherubims_ are guardians of the "_Shekinah_" ([Heb.], the glory presence of YHWH; _the Light of the world_), the **stars** (including the sun and the moon), **Eden** and the **throne of God**. _Cherubims_ also guard the "_Tree of Knowledge_." _Cherubims_ have **eternal vigilance** and **perfect knowledge** of God. _Cherubims_ **radiate the glory light** and **knowledge of God**. _Cherubims_ have **4 wings** and **4 faces**. _Cherubims_ are the **bearers of YHWH's chariot**, whenever he decides to leave the heavens and visit His created universe or the earth.

One _Cherubim_ angel is called in apocrypha _**Sachiel**_ ("The covering of God"). He is an _**angel of healing, heavenly transportation**_ and _**godly prosperity**_. _**Sachiel**_ was the angel of **1 Kings 19:5-7** restoring Elijah to his ministry assignment (Pers. Rev. GR). "And as he lay and slept under a juniper tree, behold, then **an angel** (_Sachiel_, [GR]) **touched him**, and said unto him, **Arise** and **eat**." "And the angel of the LORD (_Sachiel_, [GR]) came again the **second time**, and touched him, and said, "**Arise** and **eat**; because the journey is too great for you." Another _Cherubim_ _**Camael/Chamuel**_ ("One who sees God," more details about him see book 2), was the angel, that has **given encouragement** and **strength to Yeshua** in the **garden of Gethsemane in Jerusalem** (Luke 22:43, [Pers. Rev. GR]), reminding him of the promise of the resurrection. The _Cherubim_ _**Jophiel**_ ("Beauty of God"), mentioned in _Revelation of Moses_, was in Eden the **appointed** _**guardian**_, together with _Haniel_, of the "**tree of life**." Second, and most memorably, _Jophiel_ was together with _Camael_ when he **drove Adam** and **Eve out of** the **Garden of Eden** (see _Rev. Moses_, for more details of _Jophiel_ see book 2).

Other _Cherubims_ are: _**Aziel**_ ("Strengthened of God"), an _**angel of restoration**_. His name is linked to Exodus 15:2: "The LORD is my strength and song, and he is become my salvation." _**Azriel**_ ("Help of God"), is an **angel of restoration** and a _warrior Cherubim_. His name is linked to Exodus 18:4: "And the name of the other was Eliezer; for the God of my father, said he, was my help, and delivered me from the sword of Pharaoh:" _Azriel_ **was** the **Cherubim** who **accompanied** and **helped YHWH Echad** at the **defeat** of the **Egyptian army** at the **Red Sea** (Pers. Rev. GR, see Exodus 14:27-28). _**Azriel**_ **together** with _angels of the wind_ "**parted** the **Red Sea for Israel**," and **afterwards** "**let the waters flow back over the Egyptian army**." (Proph. Barbie Breathitt confirmed ministry of angels at Red Sea). _**Jaaziel**_ ("Emboldened of God"), is an _**angel of restoration, encouragement**_ and _**boldness**_. His name is linked to Acts 4:31: "And when they had prayed, the place was shaken where they were assembled together; and they were all filled with the Ruach HaKodesh, and they spoke the word of God with boldness." (all revelations to the last three listed _Cherubims_ are Pers. Rev. GR).

Ref.: Justin Abraham, COBH-Angel Series, 2015; Tudor Bismark, Prayer Summit, 2013; Hebrew internet source (archangel descriptions); Ahmad Bruckman, Angels in Judaism, 2015; Alfred Edersheim, Jewish Angelology and Demonology, 2015

Twelve Orders of the Angels (synergy) (XII)

10. *Ishim*-Guardians/ *Principalities (Ps. 104:4):* **Sandalphon** ("Co-brother," or "Co-worker"). Revelations below are Pers. Rev. GR, if not otherwise cited. *Sandalphon is mentioned in 3rd Enoch:* "In the camp of the *Shekinah*/Glory presence of God are *Metatron,* **Sandalphon**, *Uriel, Raphael, Michael,* and *Gabriel."* In *Revelation of Moses* is written: "Then God had to station himself in front of the fires of *Sandalphon* to allow Moses to pass safely by" (my [GR] addition: because of *Moses fear of Sandalphon* as one of the *greatest angels created). Sandalphon* is one of heavens tallest angels/ "giant," also the **leader** of the **heavenly worship bands** and *Zamarim* angels (Pers. Rev. GR). *Sandalphon* watches over the ark of the covenant. *Sandalphon* is **an** *angel of glory,* **Shalom** and *prayer,* and he is gathering/bundling prayers of the faithful, which he sends to the throne room through *Metatron. Sandalphon* watches over the **sexual moral of mankind.** *Sandalphon* himself makes or **let make crowns by** *heavenly goldsmith angels* ("*Tsaraphim angels*" [Heb.], details see book 2) for YHWH Echad and saints, including *king David* (28 "good crowns" are mentioned in the Bible). The crowns rise of their own accord. *Sandalphon* is also a **teacher of spiritual warfare** (for David see Ps. 144:1). *Sandalphon* is mentioned in **Rev. 19:10:** "I'am *Sandalphon." Sandalphon* was the angel **showing** the apostle **John the dimensions of heaven**, the **throne room, council rooms** and **court rooms** etc. (Pers. Rev. GR, analogy to *Metatron* showing the heavens to Moses and Enoch). *Sandalphon* was also an **angelic preceptor to king David** and he has **strong ministry interaction/alignment with the** *"Davidic type of apostle"* (Pers. Rev. GR).

Ishims love to praise and extol the Lord and are **made out of fire** and **snow** (*Rev. Moses*). **They engage the kingdom realm on behalf of nations.** *Ishims* are prince warrior angels of nations, they **engage the supernatural kingdom for you** and **on your behalf.** *Ishims* focus on building God's kingdom on earth. *Ishims* are full of passion for YHWH. *Ishims* are *guardian angels* of nations and **countries**, they are concerned with issues of politics, military matter, commerce and trade. *Ishims* influence **after YHWH's assignment** who will rule. *Ishims* bring **blessings from heaven to nations.** *Ishims* inspire, **when they have an assignment,** arts or sciences. They have the ability to touch the hearts and minds of mortals and **perform miracles** that are noticed, but are often inexplicable and dismissed by humankind. *Ishims* **wearing crowns** and **carrying a scepter.** Solomon said in **Proverbs 8:4** (Tanakh, [Jewish Bible]): "Unto you, O *Ishim*, I call."

One *Ishim* is called in apocrypha *Ana(h)el* ("God has answered"). *Anael* is one of the **headmasters** in **schooling other angels** (Pers. Rev. GR) and he is set as a *watching angel,* under the administration of *Sandalphon,* over everything concerning **the sexual moral/sexuality** of mankind (Pers. Rev. GR). I (GR) found out that *Anael* also **watches** over the **regulations of YHWH concerning food** ([Heb.] *"Kashrut"*), e.g. to eat clean animals (Lev. 11:1-8). **Eating unclean animals weakens** the **soul** (Lev. 20:22-26) and could allow **unclean spirits** or **fallen angels** (e.g. Apollo, Dionysus, Persephone or Tammuz), often **associated with sexual sin,** to **attack** us. In the NT apocrypha *Didache* 6:3 is written by the *"first"* **12 apostles of the lamb/ Yeshua**, that we should "*bear what we are able to fullfil*" concerning **Kashrut.** Tammuz is also called *Mithras/* e.g. the *fallen angel Galgaliel,* a fallen *Ophanim* angel, associated with the sin of homosexuality (Pers. Rev. GR).

Ref.: Justin Abraham, COBH-Angel Series, 2015; Tudor Bismark, Prayer Summit, 2013; Hebrew internet source (archangel descriptions); Ahmad Bruckman, Angels in Judaism, 2015; Alfred Edersheim, Jewish Angelology and Demonology, 2015; Kathy Madden, Crowns in the Bible, 2015; Michael K Lake, Eating God's Way, 2010

The two missing Orders of the Angels (I)

11. *Irim*-Watcher Angels/ *Qaddisim*/ Holy ones: former **Leader** Semyaza (*Book of Enoch*), now *Uriel* (Pers. Rev. GR). Revelations below are Pers. Rev. GR, if not otherwise cited. *Watchers* are mentioned in the *books of Enoch, Book of Jubilees, Rev. Moses*, and *Genesis Apocryphon* but are also mentioned *after the flood* in **Dan. 4:13, 17, 21**: (1) "I saw in the visions of my head upon my bed, and, behold, a *watcher*, **a holy one** came down from heaven;" (2) "This sentence is by the **decree of the watchers**, and the decision by the **word of the holy ones**: to the intent that the living may know that the most High rules in the kingdom of men, and gives it to whomever he will, and sets up over it the lowliest of men." (3) "And whereas the **king saw a watcher, a holy one coming down from heaven**, and saying:"

The angel *Navehiel* ("Temple of God," or "Flock of God"), is the 2nd in rank *Irim* under *Uriel* (Pers. Rev. GR). His name is linked to Ezek. 34:31: "And you my flock, the flock of my pasture, are men, and I am your God, says the Lord GOD."

Irim angels **have oversight over territories** (Deut. 32:8 [Septuagint]), **the 70 nations on earth** (Gen. 10), they **speak concerning these areas** in the **divine council** (Ps. 82), and the **courtrooms of heaven**, when **verdicts concerning nations** are **discussed** (Pers. Rev. GR). *Irims* **instructed in OT times mankind** about **judgement [justice]** and **uprightness [righteousness], in NT times this is** now the **work of the Ruach HaKodesh** (*Book of Jubilees* 4:15, John 16:8). A description of the appearance of *Irims* is given in *2nd Enoch* ch. 18: "They have ***human appearance***, and their **size (is) greater than that of great giants.**" Since 200 myriads (*2nd Enoch*) of *Irims* fell under Semyaza at the time of Jared (*1st Enoch*), I (GR) believe that at least 200 myriads of *Irims* **loyal to Yeshua** are existing now. *Irims* are **helping now with "*Evangelising*" the earth** (watching for the "*lost ones*," Ap. Tim Sheets). *Irims* also **minstering to** and **helping now godly leaders** of the **seven moutains of society, to rule** and **reign** in **justice** and **righteousness** on their **assigned mountain with godly authority** and **power** (Pers. Rev. GR). *Irims* help Yeshua that **records of iniquity** are **removed** (Pers. Rev. GR). Some scholars are saying that *Irims* are the *guardian angels* of nations, comparing them to "*guarding Cherubims*" (titled so in the "*Hebraic Roots Bible*") of the nations. In *Legends of the Jews* it is written, that "**YHWH turned** to the **70 angels who encompass His throne**, (*Irims*, [GR]), and spake:" "Go to, let us go down, and **there** (Babel, [GR]) **confound** their **language**, that they may not understand one another's speech." "It was on this occasion that YHWH and the **seventy angels** that **surround His throne cast lots concerning** the **various nations** (casting lots was a common practice in OT times, see for example Lev. 16:8). **Each angel** received **a nation, and Israel fell to** the **lot of God**. To **every nation a peculiar language** was **assigned,** Hebrew being **reserved for Israel**, the **language made use of by God** at the **creation of the world.**" But *Michael*, as already mentioned, has **delegated authority by YHWH as prince angel over Israel**. More details about the *70 angels of the nations* see book 2. Some scholars **place *Irims* in** the **hierarchy** of the **angelic orders under** the **angels mostly ministering in** the **throne room** of YHWH, e.g. *The Living Creatures, Seraphims, Cherubims*, and *Wheels*. In the *Genesis Apocryphon* (IQA poc. 2), as well as in Genesis 6:2 ff. (see also *1st Enoch* 6:8), the term *Irims* refers to "the sons of God or *Benai Elohims* (*Irims* and *Benai Elohims* are for me [GR] 2 *different angelic orders*!)."

Ref.: Greg Crawford, Angels Helping Us Contend, 2013; Dale M. Sides, Angels in the Army, 2004; Pers. Rev. GR; Makayla Ryan, Heavenly Angels, e-book 2015

The two missing Orders of the Angels (II)

12. _Zamarim_-Worshiping Spirits/ _Angels of Glory/ Parasim/ Sarim/ Shachaim:_ former **Leader** Lucifer (Ezek. 28:13, Isa. 14:12, and _2nd Enoch_), now **Sandalphon** (Pers. Rev. GR). Revelations below are Pers. Rev. GR, if not otherwise cited. _2nd Enoch:_ "He (YHWH, [GR]) created _Lucifer_, to share in the beauty of all that God created and was to create. _Lucifer_ was the angel of music and even his every step was the sound of soft tinkling cymbals. _Lucifer_ radiated the color of emeralds to reflect God's most favorite color." Ezek. 28:13: "The **workmanship** of your **timbrels** and **pipes** was prepared for you on the day you (Lucifer, [GR]) were created." **Lucifer** was **Yeshua's angel until his fall** (Ap. Tim Sheets). _Zamarims_ are mentioned in Rev. 5:11, Rev. 7:11, and _Apoc. Moses._

"The **number of** _worship angels_ ([Heb.] _Zamarim_) or **angels of glory in** heaven are (estimated to be, [GR]) **660.000** (_3rd Enoch_)."

Zamarims live **normally** in the **kingdom/dimensions of heaven(s)**. _Zamarims_ **can appear on earth** (Luke 2:13-14) or **worship before** the **throne of God**. Sometimes **a group of** _Zamarims_ or **one individual** _Zamarim_ **can be heard audibly in** the **natural during worship times** (Pers. Rev. GR). Hear for example _Jason Uptons_ song _"Fly"_ with a singing _Zamarim_ or _singing angelic choirs_ at worship CD's of Roy Fields (Personal testimony of Roy Fields at a Isaiah 60 glory conference 2018 from TOS Ministries, Tübingen, Germany).

Zamarims are made **out of fire** and **water** (_Rev. Moses_). The name _"Zamarim"_ is mentioned in Joshua 18:22 (Tanakh, [Jewish Bible]) as a city of the tribe of Benjamin. In addition to the _Seraphims_ and _Cherubims_ who mostly worship God in the throne room, **worship angels** join in worship during **Edah services. They often sit up** in the **rafters of the Edah** (Christa Kinde, [Pers. Rev. GR]). The _Zamarims_ derive their name from _"zamar"_ [Heb.], _"sing with instruments."_

Although all angels express themselves through song, _Zamarim angels_ truly **live** to **praise God** with **everything they have.** One thing that sets apart this order of musically inclined angels is **their wings,** which are designed more for beauty (**God's glory splendour on their wings,** e.g. **flames of fire,** that's why _angels of glory_) than for flight (Christa Kinde). Psalmist Roy Fields sings about _Zamarims_ in the **worship song** "In The Presence Of Angels," album "Rain Down," published 2010: "In the presence of angels **with God's glory on their wings.**"

Zamarims are also craftsmen for **manufacturing music instruments** for **heavenly worship.** Sometimes they **can bring Shofars** or **silver trumpets,** or **other instruments for worship** as gifts to saints **to equip them** for their **personal ministry** on earth (Pers. Rev. GR). **Sometimes they can bring** an **activation via trumpet blasts** from God to saints. Ap. Jeff Jansen was **activated via trumpet sounds** by them (see his book _"Revival in the secret place"_).

The angel _Israel_ ("He will rule as God"), is the _Zamarim_ who **plays a blast** upon his **mighty Shofar** to **awaken** the **slumbering dead** (link to Rev. 20:13, 1 Thess. 4:16, [Pers. Rev. GR]). _Israel_ is also a _Merkabah angel_ (more details about _Merkabah angels_ see book 2), **wearing as his weapon** a **big sword** (Pers. Rev. GR).

Ref.: Greg Crawford, Angels Helping Us Contend, 2013; Dale M. Sides, Angels In The Army, 2004; Pers. Rev. GR; Christa Kinde, Prophetic writer, artist, 2015; Makayla Ryan, Heavenly Angels, e-book 2015

The two missing Orders of the Angels (III)

12. *Zamarim-Worshiping Spirits/ Angels of Glory/ Parasim/ Sarim/ Shachaim:*

Revelations below are Pers. Rev. GR, if not otherwise cited. **Tagas** ("Mark of God"), *3rd Enoch*, is a **tall archangel** and has **50 myriads of Zamarims** (composed of three different angelic choirs, see next paragraph) directly under him. The **faces** of these *Zamarims* in worship are **directed towards** the **"Shekinah" presence** of YHWH Echad (*Rev. Moses*). **Tagas** leads the **angelic choirs** (1) **Degalim**, (2) **Sebalim**, and (3) **Gedulim** or **Gedudim**, that sing eternal praises of the Lord (*3rd Enoch*). **Degalim** ([Heb.] *"degal"* means: **flag** or **banner**) are **tall angels** worshiping YHWH Echad with **flags** and **banners**. **Sebalim**, ([Heb.] *"sebal"* means: to bear, **carry [a load]**) are *tall angels* removing *loads* or *false burdens* in a **worship atmosphere** from the worshipper. **Gedulim** ([Heb.] *"gedulah"* means: **greatness**, magnitude) are **mighty angels** **proclaiming** day and night in praise and worship *"how great is YHWH Echad,"* ([Heb.] "Gadol Elohai"). **Gedulim** angels **inspired** with their worship proclamation Chris Tomlin to write 2003 **the song** "How great is our God." These *three angelic choirs* mentioned above closely work together with **Tsinnorseraphim** ([Heb.] means: *"The Burning ones of God creating tunnels;"* [Heb.] *"tsinnor"* means: tunnel). **Tsinnorseraphims** are a *specialized group* of *Seraphim* angels, their **highest leaders** are the angels *Seraphiel* (more details about him see book 2) and **Tagas**.

In a *glory worship atmosphere* when *Gedulims* interact with *Tsinnorseraphims*, *Degalims* and *Sebalims they* create *"fire tunnels"* to **remove burdens** from the worshipper. *Gedulims* hereby **proclaim** in praise and worship the *"greatness of YHWH Echad,"* ([Heb.] "Gadol Elohai"), that "YHWH is **greater than** every **circumstance** or **trials mankind faces** in **their life on earth.**" *Degalims* **raise** their **flags** and **banners** to **create a tunnel**, *Sebalims* **lift down** from the **shoulders** of the worshippers **loads** or **false burdens** and *Tsinnorseraphims* **set** the **tunnel ablaze** with the **fire of YHWH Echad.** *Tsinnorseraphims* thereby **burn** away **iniquity, sins** and **transgressions** of the **life** of the **saints going through the tunnel.** *Revivalist Neil Gilligan*, in his book *"Surprisingly Supernatural"* (2012), describes the **formation of** such a *"fire tunnel"* by the *four angel groups* during a **ministry time** in his **house church.** Neil Gilligan only saw in the spirit one *Tsinnorseraphim* angel **minstering deliverance** and **healing to saints walking through** the *"fire tunnel."*

Shahakiel ("Bow down in worship before God"), mentioned in *3rd Enoch, is* also **one** of the **highest Zamarims**, link to Gen. 24:26: "And <u>the man bowed down his head</u>, and <u>worshiped the LORD.</u>" **Shahakiel** is the **highest specialized Zamarim angel set over** the *Shachakim, Shahakim, Shachaim,* or *Shahavim angels* (*3rd Enoch*). **Shahakiel** ministers directly under the administration of **Uriel** (Pers. Rev. GR, more of *Shachaim angels* see also **page 39**). *Shachaims* additionally are *"refiners,"* [Heb.] *"Shachaq,"* who **improve** and **regulate duties** in the **dimensions of heavens** (*3rd Enoch*). *Shachaims* **perform** their **ministry** in **constant praise** and **worship,** their **faces** kept **towards the glory of YHWH Echad** (*3rd Enoch*).

Ref.: Greg Crawford, Angels Helping Us Contend, 2013; Dale M. Sides, Angels In The Army, 2004; Pers. Rev. GR; Christa Kinde, Prophetic writer, artist, 2015; Makayla Ryan, Heavenly Angels, e-book 2015

Testament of Isaac ch. 7: "And the **angels** will be **their** (the **saints, sons** and **daughters** of the **God of Israel**, [GR]) **friends**, because of **their perfect faith** and **their purity.**"

Angels in the OT Apocrypha *Book of Gad the Seer* (mentioned in 1 Chron. 29:29)

• Gad 1:54: The angel instructing Gad is the angel *Zidkiel* ("Justice," or "Right of God") [GR]: "And the **one dressed in** (**white**) **linen** came down to me and touched me, saying:" (similar to Rev. 15:6)

• Gad 2:26: "At the end of days *Michael* the great prince will **stand up in war like a whirlwind against** the **fallen angel** Samael, a prince of this world, to **put him under** His (Yeshua's, [GR]) feet, in the wind of the LORD, and it shall be eaten up; for the LORD has spoken it." (similar to Rev. 12:7, *T. Moses* ch. 10, and link to Luke 20:43)

• Gad 5:5-6: The angel *Abdiel* punishes the Philistines: "That night, **a fire angel** ([Heb.] "*Seraphim*"), (*Abdiel*, [GR]), **came from heaven** with his **drawn sword in his hand**. And he **attacked** the **camp** of the uncircumcised. It was such a **great slaughter** that **none** of them were **left alive**." (link to 2 Sam. 5:23)

• Gad 7:20 ff.: The angel *Adbiel* punishes David's sin for counting Israel: "And **YHWH Echad sent an angel**, (*Adbiel*, [GR]), **unto Jerusalem to destroy it**; and as he was destroying it, the **LORD beheld**, and He repented Him of the evil, and **said to** the angel, (*Adbiel*, [GR]), that was destroying the people:" "It is **enough**; now **stay your hand**." (link to 1 Chron. 21:12-30)

• Gad 14:3-4: "And here is the **appearance** of the **throne: twelve stairs led up** to the **throne** (six of gold and six of silver), and there was a **square back** to the **throne**, like a **sapphire stone**. And at its right side were **three chairs** and at its left side were **four chairs** near the throne, *like the seven that see the king's face* (**the seven highest archangels of YHWH Echad**, [GR]; see *1st Enoch* 20:1-7), **covered** with **gold** and **silver** and **precious stones**." (link to Ezek. 1:26)

• Gad 14:7 ff.: The angel *Semalion* ("Breaker of God") [GR] reads the books of the last judgement of the Lord: "And **then a man dressed in** (**white**) **linen brought** before the **glory of the LORD three books** that **contained** the **records of every man**. And he read the first book and it contained the **just deeds** (*book of works/rewards*, [GR]) of **His people**." "And the **man dressed in** (**white**) **linen cried like** a **ram's horn** (e.g. a *Shofar*, [GR]), saying:" (links to Rev. 20:12, Dan. 7:10)

• Gad 14:18: The *angel of peace, Shelumiel* ("Peace of God") [GR], interacts with the seer: "Then **one** of the *Cherubims*, (*Shelumiel*, [GR]), **flew up to me** and **he put an olive leaf** on **my mouth**, and **said**, "Lo, this has touched your mouth, and **your iniquity** is **taken away**, and your **sin forgiven**." (similar to Isaiah 6:6)

• For **more details** of the **specific angels called by name** see book 2!

Pers. Rev. GR

Michael prophecies in *Jos. Asen.* 15:6 about the **descendants of** the patriarch **Joseph** (also a **prophetic picture** of **Yeshua**, or of **Israel** and of **Zion**, [GR]): "For **many nations shall take refuge** in you, and **under your wings** shall **many peoples find shelter**, and **within your walls** those who **give their allegiance to YHWH Echad** in **repentance** will **find security**." (links to: Psalm 91, Psalm 61:3, Psalm 9:9, Psalm 122:7, and Matt. 11:28-30)

Angels in the OT Apocrypha *The Testaments of the Twelve Patriarchs*

• In *the Testament of Reuben* 3:15: "And forthwith <u>an angel of God</u>, (*Netsachiel*, [GR]), revealed to my father concerning my impiety." (see Gen. 35:22); 5:3: "...the <u>angel of the Lord</u>, (*Netsachiel*, [GR]), told me, and taught me, that…" (*angels preaching* see Gal. 1:8)

• In *the Testament of Simeon* 2:8-9: "But his God and the God of his fathers <u>sent forth His angel</u>, (*Paltiel* ["Deliverance of God"], [GR]), and **delivered him** out of my hands." (similar to Acts 12:7)

• In *the whole Testament of Levi*, **Michael** was mentioned, for example in ch. 3: "And behold the heavens were opened and an <u>angel of God</u>, (*Michael*, [GR]), <u>said to me</u>:" "Levi enter." The archangel *Michael* was **showing Levi** the **dimensions of heavens** and **giving him a shield** and **a sword**. (similar to *1st Enoch*)

• In *the Testament of Judah* 3:10: "For he saw in a vision concerning me that <u>an angel of might</u> (<u>[Heb.] *Erelim*</u>), (*Tzaphkiel*, [GR]), followed me everywhere, that I **should not be overcome**." (see Ps. 103:20); 10:3: "And on the third night <u>an angel of the Lord</u>, (*Hamuel* ["Anger of God"], [GR]), **smote him** (the man ER, [GR])." (similar to *Supplement* to Daniel ch. 13:59 [Septuagint]); 15:5-6: "And the <u>angel of God</u>, (*Netsachiel*, [GR]), <u>showed me</u> that for ever do **women bear rule** over king and beggar alike." (link to 1 Kings 21:7); 21:5: "For the <u>angel of the Lord</u>, (*Bethiel* ["House of God"], [GR]), <u>said unto me</u>." 26:2: "And the Lord blessed Levi, and <u>the *angel of the presence*</u>, (*Phanuel*, [GR]), **blessed me** (Judah, [GR])." (similar to Gen. 48:16, *Jos. Asen.* 16:7, 17:5, and *T. Jac.* ch. 6: "The **angel** (*Michael*, [GR]) who **rescues me** from all **my tribulations** (see *T. Jac.* in book 2 of this series), **bless** these **lads** who are my sons." (*Angels blessing* see **page 12** and **page 24**)

• In *the Testament of Issachar* 2:1: "Then <u>appeared to Jacob an angel of the Lord</u>, (*Uriel*, [GR]), saying." (similar to Gen. 31:11)

• In *the Testament of Dan* 5:4: "For <u>an angel of the Lord</u>, (*Michael*, [GR]), shall guide them both." (similar to Num. 20:16); 6:2-3: "Draw near unto God and <u>unto the angel</u>, (*Michael*, [GR]), <u>that interceded for you</u>, for he is a <u>mediator (intercessory, [GR]) angel</u> between God and man, and for the **peace of Israel** he shall stand up against the kingdom of the enemy." (see *1st Enoch*); 6:5: "For the very *angel of peace*, (*Shelumiel*, [GR]), shall **strengthen Israel**, that it fall not into the extremity of evil." (see *1st Enoch*)

• In *the Testament of Asher* 6:6: "But if he is **peaceful with joy** <u>he meeteth the *angel of peace*</u>, (*Shelumiel*, [GR]), and he **leadeth him into** the **eternal life of paradise**." (see *1st Enoch*)

• In *the Testament of Joseph* 6:6: "Now therefore know that the God of my father <u>hath revealed unto me by His angel</u>, (*Raziel*, [GR]), thy wickedness." (similar to Rev. 1:1); 6:7: "The God of my fathers <u>and the angel of Abraham</u>, (*Gabriel*, [GR]), **be with me** and **ate**." (similar to Gen. 18:2)

• In *the Testament of Benjamin* 6:1-2: "for the *angel of peace*, (*Shelumiel*, [GR]), **guideth** his **soul to paradise**." (see *1st Enoch*)

• For **more details** of the **specific angels called by name** see book 2!

Angels in the NT Apocrypha *Apocalypse of Paul* (I)

• *Simiel* ("Appointed by God"), [GR] ch. 1 to ch. 51 **speaks** to Paul and **guides him** on his **journey** through *Heaven* and *Sheol*. (similar to *1ˢᵗ Enoch*)

• Ch. 7- ch. 10: Speech of the *personal guardian angels*, appearing before the throne of YHWH Echad: "The *personal, guardian angels* **present** all the **work which every man hath wrought**." (similar to *3ʳᵈ Baruch* ch. 13)

• Ch. 11: *Simiel* announces to Paul, that he will show him on his **journey with him**, the *Heavens* and *Sheol*, and the different **places of blessings for** the **saints** and **punishments for** the **sinners**. (similar to *1ˢᵗ Enoch*)

• Ch. 11: *Angels of punishment* (as in *Apoc. of Zephania* 4:3) are described.

• Ch. 12: *Angels of justice* or *righteousness* are described: "Whose **faces shone like** the **sun**, and their **loins** were **girt with golden girdles**, **holding palms** in their **hands**, and the **sign of YHWH Echad on them**, **clad** in **raiment** whereon was **written the name** of the **Son of YHWH Echad (Yeshua, [GR])**; these angels are **full of** all **gentleness** and **mercy**." (similar to *Jos. Asen.* 14:9)

• Ch. 13ff.: *Simiel* shows Paul the time of **death of saints** and **sinners** and **their trials** before the **courts of heaven**. *Guardian angels* must **testify before** the **courts of heaven** about the **life of their alloted humans**. (similar to *3ʳᵈ Baruch* ch. 13, Rev. 20:12, and Dan. 7:10)

• Ch. 14: *Michael* (here mentioned as an *angel of the covenant*) and *myriads of angels* are present when **YHWH Echad** looks for *fruits of righteousness* **from** the **saints** or when He, YHWH, *judges* the **sinners**. (see Heb. 12:22, *3ʳᵈ Baruch* ch. 13)

• Ch. 16: A **verdict** was rendered by **YHWH Echad** to **hand** the **sinner over** to the *angel of punishment Temeluch* ("God's caretaker angel"). (similar to *Apoc. of Zephania* 4:3)

• Ch. 17: Two *bailiff angels* (*Asariel* ("Right of God, whom God has bound"), and *Daniel* ("Judge of God"), [GR]) **bring** the **soul of a deceased one** before the **judgement seat** of **YHWH Echad**. (see 2 Cor. 5:10)

• Ch. 18: After the **trial** is **finished**, the **sinner** is **handed over** again to the *angel of punishment Temeluch*. (similar to *Apoc. of Zephania* 4:3)

• Ch. 19: *Simiel* now shows Paul the *dimensions of heaven*. (similar to *1ˢᵗ Enoch*)

• Ch. 22: *Michael* **brings** the **saints** into the **city** of **Yeshua HaMashiach**. (similar to Jude 1:9)

• Ch. 25: *Michael* **brings** the **prophets of YHWH Echad** through the *path of the prophets* into the *place of prophets* within the **city** of **Yeshua HaMashiach**. The *river of honey* **flows** near the *place of prophets* in heaven. (similar to *1ˢᵗ Enoch*)

• Ch. 30: "**Alleluia** is spoken in **Hebrew**, that is the **speech of YHWH Echad** and of the **angels** of **YHWH Echad**."

• For **more details** of the **specific angels called by name** see book 2!

Angels in the NT Apocrypha *Apocalypse of Paul* (II)

• Ch. 31: *Simiel* now shows Paul the different compartments of **Sheol/Hell**. (similar to *1ˢᵗ Enoch*)

• Ch. 34: *The angel of punishment Aftemelouchos* ("Cast with no regret into the hell fire"), is described and also *other angels of punishment*. (similar to *Apoc. of Zephania* 4:3)

• Ch. 36: The angel *Hayliel* ("Calamity of God"), is **punishing a sinner**: "Then the *angel that was over the torments* (*Hayliel*, [GR]) came, having a **great razor, red-hot**, and therewith he cut the lips of that man and the tongue likewise." (similar to *Apoc. of Zephania* 4:3)

• Ch. 39: *Four angels of punishment* (also **mentioned** in **Rev. 9:14**, [Pers. Rev. GR]) (*Dalkiel* ["God is strong in my weakness"], *Shoftiel* ["The judge of God"], *Hutriel* ("The rod of God"), and *Puriel* ["The fire of God"], [GR]) punish a sinner: "*Four fearful angels* holding in *their hands red-hot chains*, and they *put them upon their necks* and **led them away into darkness**." (similar to *Apoc. of Zephania* 4:3)

• Ch. 40: *The angel of punishment Aftemelouchos reads the verdicts of eternal punishment over sinners*: "**Laying most fierce torments** upon them and saying." (similar to *Apoc. of Zephania* 4:3)

• Ch. 40-41: Again *angels of punishment* are *mentioned*: "Angels *having horns of fire* constrained **them** and **smote them** and **closed up their nostrils**, saying unto them:" (similar to *Apoc. of Zephania* 4:3)

• Ch. 41: The *gatekeeper angel Rabakiel* ("Breastplate of God") [GR], *opens the deeper layers* of **Sheol**, e.g. the *Abyss*, unto Paul for the **next** "sightseeing **tour**." (similar to *1ˢᵗ Enoch*)

• Ch. 43: After the *deep travail* and *intercession* of *Paul about the torments* of Sheol, *Michael* shows up at the **entrance** of the **Abyss**, and *Michael explains* to the *sinners* that "*after the death of a man, he can not make intercession for them before* the **throne of YHWH Echad** as he did as *angel of intercession while they lived*." (similar to *1ˢᵗ Enoch* and see Heb. 9:27)

• Ch. 44: Now **Yeshua HaMashiach appears** and **speaks of His blood**, which was **shed for** the **sins of all mankind**, but the **sinners refused** to **accept His** *gift of salvation* on the **cross of Calvary, so they must stay in** *Sheol*. (see book of Heb.)

• Ch. 45 ff.: *Simiel* **shows Paul** now the "*Paradise*" **with all** the **heroes of faith**, the **saints** and the **patriarchs of Israel**. (similar to *1ˢᵗ Enoch*)

• Ch. 48: Paul now sees *Michael*, **all the angels** and **archangels weeping over the Son of God, Yeshua HaMashiach**, that was **hanging as a sinless man on the cross**. (you can see with your spiritual eyes in the glory realm back and forth in space and time, [GR])

• Ch. 49: *Simiel* said: "Every one of the saints hath *his own angel*, that *standeth by him* and *singeth hymns*, and the *one departeth not from the other*." (details for *Hadarim* angels on **page 18** and in book 2)

• For **more details** of the **specific angels called by name** see book 2!

Angels in the NT Apocrypha *Revelation of John*

• Ch. 11: "Then will I send forth mine (**Yeshua's**, [GR]) *angels*, and they **shall take the ram's horns** (e.g. *Shofars*, [GR]) that lie upon the cloud; and *Michael* and *Gabriel* shall go forth out of the heaven and **sound with those horns**, as the prophet David foretold, **with** the **voice of** a **trumpet of horn** (e.g. a *Shofar*, [GR])." (see Rev. 8:6)

• Ch. 16: "All the **human race shall arise without earthly bodies**, as I told you that in the **resurrection** they **neither marry** nor are **given in marriage**, but **are as the** *angels* **of YHWH Echad**." (see Mark 12:25)

• Ch. 20: "Then will I **send** forth mine (**Yeshua's**, [GR]) *angels* **over** the **face** of **all the earth**, and they **shall lift off the earth**, everything **honourable**, and everything **precious**." (see Rev. 14:15)

• Ch. 23: "Then shall I **send** forth mine (**Yeshua's**, [GR]) *angels* over the **face** of **all the earth**, and **they shall burn up the earth**." (see 2 Pet. 3:7)

• Ch. 28: "Then will I send an *angel*, (*Uriel*, [GR]), out of heaven, and he shall **cry with a loud voice**, saying: Hear, O earth, and be strong, saith the Lord; for I am coming down to thee. And the **voice of the** *angel*, (*Uriel*, [GR]), **shall be heard** from the **one end of the world** even to the other, and **even to** the **remotest part of the abyss**." "…and **an innumerable multitude of** *angels* **shall come down to** the **earth**." (similar to Rev. 14:18)

• Ch. 29: "And then there shall **go before me** (**Yeshua**, [GR]) *myriads of angels* and **archangels**, *bearing my throne*, crying out, Holy, holy, holy, *Lord of Sabaoth*; *heaven* and *earth are full of Thy glory*." (see Heb. 12:22, Isaiah 6:2, and Rev. 4:8)

• Ch. 33: "And all the *multitudes of the angels* will answer, give this *book to the Lamb* to *open it*." (see Rev. 5:5)

• Ch. 42: "Then the race of the *followers of the Mashiach* shall be examined, who **have received baptism** ([Heb.] "*Tevilah*"); and then the **righteous** shall **come** at **my** (**Yeshua's**, [GR]) **command**, and *the angels* (*of harvest* [GR]) *shall go* and *collect* them from *among the sinners*" (see Rev. 14:15). For "*Tevilah*" as a **sign of salvation** see Mark 16:16: "He that **believeth** and **is baptized** shall be **saved**; but he that **believeth not** shall be **damned**." Proph. Madelene Eayrs speaks of **salvation** like the **conceiving** of the baby and of **baptism** like the **birth** of the baby.

• Ch. 50: "**As great as** is the *multitude* of the *angels*, **so great is** the **race of men**, as the prophet has said: He set **bounds** to the **nations** according to the *number of the angels* of **YHWH Echad**." (see Deut. 32:8 [Septuagint])

• Ch. 52: "And **other sheep I have**, which are **not of this fold**, that is, **men who** have been **made like the** *angels* through their excellent course of life." (see John 10:16)

• For **more details** of the **specific angels called by name** see book 2!

Recommendations

Jerame Nelson: *Encountering Angels* (2015)

Justin Abraham: *COBH-Angel Series* (2015), available as MP3 set

Tudor Bismark: *Book summarizing Prayer Summit* (2013)

Marie Chapian: *Angels in Our Lives* (2013)

Judith MacNutt: *Angels* (2012), also available in German (Glory World Medien)

Greg Crawford: *Angels Helping Us Contend* (2013)

Douglas Connelly: *Angels Around Us* (1994); available also in German (CMF Verlag); *Workbook "Angels"* (Intervarsity Press) (2004)

Dale M. Sides: *Angels in the Army* (2004)

Matthew Bunson: *Angels A to Z: A Who's Who of the Heavenly Host* (1996) (**Angelic dictionary**)

Kevin Basconi: ***Angel series*** and "***School workbooks***: *Boot camp* and *Advanced*" about angels (from different years); available in German "Mit den Engeln tanzen, Band 1-3," Glory World Medien (2015-2017)

Michael van Vlynen: *Angelic visitations*, in German "Begegnungen mit Engeln" (2015) (Verlag Gemeinde Rinteln)

Andy Angel: "*Angels: Ancient Whispers of Another World*" (2012) (**Jewish** and **early Edah/Ekklesia original literature**, **OT**, **NT**, **Apocrypha**, etc.)

Dr. A. Nyland: *Ancient Angels A-Z* (2015) (**Teaching about angels from original literature**)

Tim Sheets: *Angel Armies* (2016) (**Teaching about angels** plus **prayer decrees to activate angelic ministry at different levels**)

Jennifer Le Claire: *Angels on Assignment Again* (2017) (**Special focus on activating different kinds of angels**)

Dr. Barbie L Breathitt: *Angels in God's Kingdom* (2018) (**Teaching about angels from the books of the Bible** and **prophetic revelations about angels**)

Specific Apocrypha: *Book of Enoch, Book of Jubilees, Book of Jasher, Book of Gad the Seer*, the *2nd-4th Book of Ezra*, Dead Sea scrolls: "*War Rules of Israel*," *The Testaments of the 12 Patriarchs*, Book *Apocalypse of Paul*, and Book *Apocalypse of John*.

Michael in *Jos. Asen.* 15:2, 6: "Take heart, Aseneth, for lo, the Lord has **heard** the **words of your confession**. Take heart, Aseneth, **your name is written** in the **book of life**, and it will **never be blotted out**. From today you will **be made new**, and **refashioned**, and **given new life**; and you shall **eat** the **bread of life** and **drink** the **cup of immortality**, and **be anointed** with the unction of **incorruption**." "And you shall **no more** be **called** Aseneth, but "*City of Refuge*" shall be **your name**." (links to: Rom. 10:10, 2 Cor. 5:17, Rev. 3:5, John 6:35, John 7:37, 1 Pet. 1:21, and Rev. 2:17)

Prayers to activate angels ("*War Rules of Israel*")

Before I list the respective four prayers, let me first introduce you to the fascinating story about the "*War rules of Israel.*" The prayers mentioned in the whole "*War rules of Israel,*" were *prayed by all the priests* and the *soldiers of Israel* since "the time of Abraham" until the "time of the prophet Malachi" **before** the **army of the Israelites went into battle** against their **natural** and **spiritual enemies**. The "*War rules of Israel*" manuscripts were packed away by Essene scribes in Qumram caves about 150 B.C.. The "*War rules of Israel*" were YHWH Echad's Ruach HaKodesh-inspired *step by step* **prayer manual**, based on 19 separate actions, for the army of the children of Israel to be **victorious** in battle **through** the **ministry** of **angels of YHWH Echad**. The "*War rules of Israel*" illustrate the **attitude** and **qualifications** for **soldiers**, proper **battle equipment**, **war strategy** and the **procedure** for **sending angels of the Lord** into battle. The "*War rules of Israel*" scrolls were **among** the **first found** and **restored** manuscripts from the caves of Qumram. I got the prophetic revelation by Ruach HaKodesh that the angel *Uriel* **brought Abram** (later Abraham) the "*War rules of Israel*" scrolls as **wedding gift of Yeshua** to His **bride Israel, during covenant making** with **YHWH Echad** (see Gen. 15:5ff.), because since that time enemies came against the nation Israel.

One should not forget, that **fallen angels** and **demons** also **supported** the **enemy forces** in their **war against Israel**, through **rituals, sacrifices** or **prayers** done **to them as "gods"** **before** or **during** the **ongoing battle**. In one recorded case in the Bible a **human sacrifice** of the **first born son** of the *King of Moab* **released victory** for the **enemy forces over Israel** (see 2 Kings 3:27), even they had **a prophetic word** from the prophet **Elisha to be victorious**, see 2 Kings 3:18: "He (YHWH, [GR]) will **deliver** the **Moabites** also **into your hand**."

But it is important to mention here, that when sins, transgressions or iniquity were done by Israel, the prayers in "*War rules of Israel*" had **no effect to bring victory** (for example see Josh. 7:1), because **sin separates Israel from God** and the **accuser of the breathen** has a **legal right** in the **courts of heaven** to **block the promised victory against** the **natural** and **spiritual enemies**.

Here are the four prayers activating the angels of YHWH Echad for spiritual battle:

• 1QM 9: "They shall write on all the shields of the towers: on the first, *Michael*, on the second *Gabriel*, on the third *Sariel*, and on the fourth *Raphael* (or alternatively *Raguel*, [GR]). *Michael* and *Gabriel* shall stand on the right, and *Sariel* and *Raphael* (or alternatively *Raguel*, [GR]) on the left and they shall set an ambush to (defeat our enemies, [GR])." (for *Raguel* see comment on **page 19**)

• 1QM 12: "For the multitude of the Holy Ones is with Thee (YHWH, [GR]) in heaven, and the host of angels is in Thy (YHWH, [GR]) holy abode, praising Thy (YHWH, [GR]) Name. And thou hast established in an Edah for Thyself (YHWH, [GR]) the elect of Thy (YHWH, [GR]) holy people."

• 1QM 12: "Thou (YHWH, [GR]) wilt muster the hosts of Thine (YHWH, [GR]) elect, in their Thousands and Myriads, with Thy (YHWH, [GR]) Holy Ones and with all Thine (YHWH, [GR]) angels, that they may be mighty in battle, and may smite the rebels of the earth by Thy (YHWH, [GR]) great judgements, and that they may triumph together with the elect of heaven."

• 1QM 12: "Valiant warriors of the angelic host are among our numbered men, and the Hero of War (Yeshua HaMashiach, [GR]) is with our congregation ([Heb. "*Edah*"], the host of His (Yeshua HaMashiach's, [GR]) spirits is with our foot-soldiers and horsemen."

Ref.: Dale Sides, Angels in the Army (War Rules of Israel), 2004

Prayer to interact with angels

"Lord open my eyes to the angels that are found in your word. Teach me, as I read your word, how to recognize angelic beings in the Bible when they are moving around me. Cause me to be aware of the reality of the angelic realm."

"Send your angels on assignment to help bring promises of God to pass in my life and in my family's lives, as well. Lord, help me to become aware of Heaven's help around me. Help me to see the opportunities and individuals around me, in which and for whom I can partner with the angels of Heaven to release Your manifest presence in those situations and on those people."

"Lord, loose the angels of Heaven on my behalf and bring breakthrough into every area of my life. In Yeshua HaMashiach's Mighty Name, do I pray. Amen, Amen and Amen."

Ref.: Jerame Nelson, Encountering Angels, 2015

Prayer to recieve the gift of salvation

If you are not born again, yet, and the teachings in this book, especially the descriptions of the torments for sinners and the place Sheol/Hell, mentioned in the apocrypha *"The Apocalypse of Paul"* has touched your heart and you want to be sure that you spend eternity in heaven, together with YHWH Echad, the Edah in heaven and on earth, and all the myriads of angels of Adonai, it is now the "kairos" time (see 2 Cor. 6:2) to pray loud the following prayer and **recieve** the **gift of salvation** in **Yeshua HaMashiach**.

"Dear Yeshua, come into my heart as Lord and Saviour. Forgive me of my sins, transgressions and iniquities. Wash me and cleanse me. Set me free Yeshua, thank you that you died for me. I believe that you are risen from the dead and that You're coming back again for me. Fill me with your Ruach HaKodesh. Give me a passion for the lost, a hunger for the things of YHWH Echad, a hunger to read your word, and a holy boldness to preach the gospel of Yeshua HaMashiach. I decree now: "I'm saved, I'm born again, I'm forgiven and I'm on my way to Heaven because I have Yeshua in my heart." (adapted from "The Gospel Soul Winning script," by Revivalist Rodney Howard Brown, Revival Ministries International, USA)

Congratulations, you are now a child of YHWH Echad!!!

Now it is mandatory to purchase a *good Bible version* (for example *"The One New Man Bible,"* recommended by many messianic leaders) to **study/read God's word day by day** and to **search** for a *bible believing*, *spirit filled* **Ekklesia** in your city or region, **to grow** as **child** and **disciple** of YHWH into all YHWH Echad has for your life as a son or daughter of the most high God.

The Priestly Blessing (Numbers 6:24-26)

"YHWH bless you, and keep you."

"YHWH make his face shine on you, and be gracious unto you."

"YHWH lift up his countenance upon you, and give you peace."

Y'vah-reh-k'khah YAHWEH v'yeesh-m'reh-khah
yah-ayr YAHWEH pah-nahv ay-leh-khah
vee-khoo-neh-khah.
yee-sah YAHWEH pah-nahv ay-leh-khah
v'yah-saym l'khah shalom

יברכך יהוה וישמרך
יאר יהוה פניו אליך ויחנך
ישא יהוה פניו אליך וישם לך שלום

"YHWH will kneel before you presenting gifts and will guard you with a hedge of protection."

"YHWH will illuminate the wholeness of his being toward you bringing order and he will give you comfort and sustenance."

"YHWH will lift up his wholeness of being and look upon you and he will set in place all you need to be whole and complete."

Image by Pixabay, public domain.

Pers. Rev. GR

About the Author

Dr. Apostle Gunter Rappl, born 1969, is the founding Apostle of Ekklesia Consuming Fire & GFC in Cologne, North Rhine Westfalia, Germany.

Gunter's heart beats that every single disciple of Yeshua HaMashiach through intimacy with YHWH Echad finds his God-given Identity and then makes his calling and election in the Edah Yeshua HaMashiach's sure. YHWH Echad had revealed to him some years ago the vision for the Edah/Ekklesia Consuming Fire & GFC, Cologne, in a catchword. "Delivered-Healed-Ordained and Comissioned into ministry."

After giving his life a second time to Yeshua at the month of Cheshvan 2001, he joined 2003 as a living stone an Apostolic-Prophetic Ekklesia in Cologne, followed by baptism in the spirit and in water around Purim 2003. Afterwards Dr. Apostle Gunter Rappl attended, beginning 2004 until 2010, in Germany and in the USA different bible-based training seminaries at apostolic and prophetic training centers with the focus on practical application of the studied material. He graduated 2006 sucessfully from a "School of the Prophets" (Pastors Bruno and Claudia Zimmerli, FCG Hanau, Hessen, Germany) and 2011 from a "School of Apostolic Ministries" (Apostle Randy Clark, Apostolic Equipping Institute, Spirit of Life Ministries, FL, USA). At the fall feasts 2011, Gunter was ordained and comissioned by Pastor Kay Tolman (Restoration Gateway Ministries, OR, USA) and her apostolic team as Apostle. At the end of 2013 Gunter completed the leadership training for "Advanced Deliverance Training" with the title "Train the Trainers" (Michael and Madelene Eayrs, Just like Him Ministries, GA, USA).

At the autumn feasts of Adonai 2012 Ekklesia Consuming Fire, Cologne, Germany was born in the spirit through the Ruach HaKodesh and founded by Gunter in the natural as an international apostolic, prophetic and messianic training center (Edah) based on Acts 2 and 4. On the first apostolic and prophetic conference around the spring feasts of Adonai Nissan 2013 in Cologne the calling, vision, and mandate of the Ekklesia was judged and confirmed by the attending apostles and prophets from all over the world with whom Gunter is aligned in friendship.

Since Gunter understands the safeguard of being under spiritual authority he aligned 2014 himself and the Ekklesia Consuming Fire, Cologne, with Apostle Jeff Jansen (Global Fire Ministries, TN, USA) and Ekklesia Consuming Fire became a part of the world-wide apostolic network "Global Connect" (Apostle Jeff Jansen). Around Shavuot 2015 Gunter was ordained and comissioned as Apostle in "Global Connect" by Apostle Peter Wagner, Apostle Dutch Sheets and last but not least Apostle Jeff Jansen. Since Shavuot 2015 Ekklesia Consuming Fire is the Global Fire Church, Cologne, also. Other alignments of Gunter and Ekklesia Consuming Fire & GFC, Cologne, exist to "Global Legacy" (Apostle Bill Johnson) and to the "Impact Network" (Apostle John Eckhardt), as well as to different houses, churches and ministries in Cologne, in Germany and internationally.

Additionally Gunter has a PhD in Biology and he had published around 50 articles as first or co-author in scientific peer-reviewed journals about the pathology of immune-related diseases. He always had searched for translational approaches of his research leading into medical therapies. Since the last years Gunter is in love with the "Healing oils of the bible," which not only heal through the restoring power of the Ruach HaKodesh, but are also suitable for cooking Jewish dishes (chocolates with biblical oils are a delight also).